Supporting Children with Autistic Spectrum Disorders

This practical resource contains a wealth of valuable advice and tried-and-tested strategies for identifying children and young people with autistic spectrum disorders (ASD). This fully updated text describes the different types of difficulties experienced by pupils with ASD and helps practitioners to understand their diverse needs. This fully updated new edition explores key topics, including:

- Organising the classroom and support staff
- Home – school liaison and working with siblings
- Transition to adulthood
- Independence skills
- Whole school implications

Now fully updated in line with the 2014 SEND Code of Practice, this invaluable guide provides guidance and practical strategies for teachers and other professionals, helping them to feel more confident and be more effective in supporting learners in a variety of settings. For professional development, this book also provides materials for in-house training sessions and features useful checklists, templates and photocopiable/downloadable resources.

Elizabeth Morling – Series Editor, SEN Consultant and former Head of the Education Service for Physical Disability, Hull City Council, UK

Colleen O'Connell – Assistant Headteacher at Northcott School.

Other titles published in association with the National Association for Special Educational Needs (nasen):

Language for Learning in the Secondary School: A practical guide for supporting students with speech, language and communication needs
Sue Hayden and Emma Jordan
2012/pb: 978-0-415-61975-2

Using Playful Practice to Communicate with Special Children
Margaret Corke
2012/pb: 978-0-415-68767-6

The Equality Act for Educational Professionals: A simple guide to disability and inclusion in schools
Geraldine Hills
2012/pb: 978-0-415-68768-3

More Trouble with Maths: A teacher's complete guide to identifying and diagnosing mathematical difficulties
Steve Chinn
2012/pb: 978-0-415-67013-5

Dyslexia and Inclusion: Classroom Approaches for Assessment, Teaching and Learning, second edition
Gavin Reid
2012/pb: 978-0-415-60758-2

Promoting and Delivering School-to-School Support for Special Educational Needs: A practical guide for SENCOs
Rita Cheminais
2013/pb 978-0-415-63370-3

Time to Talk: Implementing outstanding practice in speech, language and communication
Jean Gross
2013/pb: 978-0-415-63334-5

Curricula for Teaching Children and Young People with Severe or Profound and Multiple Learning Difficulties: Practical strategies for educational professionals
Peter Imray and Viv Hinchcliffe
2013/pb: 978-0-415-83847-4

Successfully Managing ADHD: A handbook for SENCOs and teachers
Fintan O'Regan
2014/pb: 978-0-415-59770-8

Brilliant Ideas for Using ICT in the Inclusive Classroom, second edition
Sally McKeown and Angela McGlashon
2015/pb: 978-1-138-80902-4

Boosting Learning in the Primary Classroom: Occupational therapy strategies that really work with pupils
Sheilagh Blyth
2015/pb: 978-1-13-882678-6

Beating Bureaucracy in Special Educational Needs, 3ed
Jean Gross
2015/pb: 978-1-138-89171-5

Transforming Reading Skills in the Secondary School: Simple strategies for improving literacy
Pat Guy
2015/pb: 978-1-138-89272-9

Supporting Children with Speech and Language Difficulties, second edition
Cathy Allenby, Judith Fearon-Wilson, Sally Merrison and Elizabeth Morling
2015/pb: 978-1-138-85511-3

Supporting Children with Dyspraxia and Motor Co-ordination Difficulties, second edition
Susan Coulter, Lesley Kynman, Elizabeth Morling, Rob Grayson and Jill Wing
2015/pb: 978-1-138-85507-6

Developing Memory Skills in the Primary Classroom: A complete programme for all
Gill Davies
2015/pb: 978-1-138-89262-0

Language for Learning in the Primary School: A practical guide for supporting pupils with language and communication difficulties across the curriculum, 2ed
Sue Hayden and Emma Jordan
2015/pb: 978-1-138-89862-2

Supporting Children with Autistic Spectrum Disorders, second edition
Elizabeth Morling and Colleen O'Connell
2016/pb: 978-1-138-85514-4

Understanding and Supporting Pupils with Moderate Learning Difficulties in the Secondary School: A practical guide
Rachael Hayes and Pippa Whittaker
2016/pb: 978-1-138-01910-2

Assessing Children with Specific Learning Difficulties: A teacher's practical guide
Gavin Reid, Gad Elbeheri and John Everatt
2016/pb: 978-0-415-67027-2

Supporting Children with Down's Syndrome, second edition
Lisa Bentley, Ruth Dance, Elizabeth Morling, Susan Miller and Susan Wong
2016/pb: 978-1-138-91485-8

Provision Mapping and the SEND Code of Practice: Making it work in primary, secondary and special schools, second edition
Anne Massey
2016/pb: 978-1-138-90707-2

Supporting Children with Medical Conditions, second edition
Susan Coulter, Lesley Kynman, Elizabeth Morling, Francesca Murray, Jilll Wang and Rob Grayson
2016/pb: 978-1-13-891491-9

Supporting Children with Autistic Spectrum Disorders

Second Edition

**Elizabeth Morling and
Colleen O'Connell**

LONDON AND NEW YORK

Helping Everyone Achieve ■■■

This edition published 2015
by Routledge
2 Park Square, Milton Park, Abingdon, Oxon OX14 4RN

and by Routledge
711 Third Avenue, New York, NY 10017

Routledge is an imprint of the Taylor & Francis Group, an informa business

First published in 2004 by David Fulton Publishers

British Library Cataloguing-in-Publication Data
A catalogue record for this book is available from the British Library

Library of Congress Cataloging in Publication Data
Morling, Elizabeth.
Supporting children with autistic spectrum disorders / Elizabeth Morling and Colleen O'Connell. – Second edition.
pages cm
1. Autistic children–Education. 2. Autism in children. I. O'Connell, Colleen. II. Title.
LC4717.M67 2015
371.9–dc23
2014047321

ISBN: 978-1-138-85513-7 (hbk)
ISBN: 978-1-138-85514-4 (pbk)
ISBN: 978-1-315-72052-4 (ebk)

Typeset in Helvetica
by Cenveo Publisher Services

MIX
Paper from
responsible sources
FSC® C013604

Printed and bound by CPI Group (UK) Ltd, Croydon, CR0 4YY

Contents

Foreword

This book was initially produced in partnership with services based in Hull, the Special Educational Needs Support Service, the Hull City Psychological Service, the Northcott ASD Outreach Service and the Hull and East Riding Community Health NHS Trust and written by:

Colleen O'Connell:	Northcott ASD outreach teacher
Ruth Dance:	Educational psychologist
Ven Delasaux:	Children's centre nursery classroom
Elizabeth Morling:	Early years transition co-ordinator
Susan Miller:	Senior educational psychologist
Kathryn Ranby:	Speech and language therapist
Pauline Russell:	Portage supervisor
Carole Stitt:	Educational psychologist
Karen Stockman:	Speech and language therapist

Edited by Colleen O'Connell, Elizabeth Morling and Carole Stitt

With thanks to senior adviser John Hill for his support and encouragement throughout the development of this series.

This book has now been updated to reflect recent legislation and current teaching practices by:

Colleen O'Connell; Assistant Head, Northcott School
Elizabeth Morling; SEN Consultant, Series Editor.

With thanks to:

Julie Bottomley, TA at Withernsea Primary School
Hannah Mackley and Pippa Berry – ASD Outreach Teachers (Northcott School) for their invaluable contributions.

It is one of a series providing an up-to-date overview of special educational needs for SENCOs, teachers, other professionals and parents.

The aim of these books is to raise awareness and address many of the issues involved in creating inclusive environments.

Owing to the nature of the difficulties presented by the condition of an ASD, it is inevitable that there are overlaps between the discrete areas of the book. The authors feel that it would be of benefit to the reader for certain points to be re-emphasised as the book is to be dipped into as necessary.

Introduction

Unlike pupils with obvious physical or sensory impairments, autism is often hidden. Staff naturally make adjustments for pupils who are deaf or blind or who cannot walk, but can unwittingly expect pupils on the autism spectrum to manage in the classroom and at break and lunchtimes without any adjustment or support. Donna Williams, an autistic adult, says that asking her to work in a group (with high social and sensory demands) is the equivalent of asking a wheelchair user to get up and walk.

(National Autistic Society)

An increasing number of pupils are diagnosed as being on the autistic spectrum, the majority of whom are in mainstream schools and academies. The following legislation gives guidance to these settings and should ensure that pupils' needs are fully met.

Definition of disability under the Equality Act 2010

A person is defined as being disabled if they have a physical or mental impairment that has a 'substantial' and 'long-term' negative effect on their ability to do normal daily activities.

Disability rights

It is against the law for a school or other education provider to treat disabled pupils/ students unfavourably. This includes:

- 'direct discrimination', e.g. refusing admission to a pupil because of a disability;
- 'indirect discrimination';
- 'discrimination arising from a disability', e.g. preventing a pupil from taking part in a school visit because of their disability;
- 'harassment', e.g. addressing a student inappropriately because they have not understood an instruction due to their disability;
- 'victimisation', suspending a disabled pupil because they have complained about harassment.

Reasonable adjustments

An educational provider has a duty to make 'reasonable adjustments' to ensure that disabled students are not discriminated against. These changes could include providing extra support and aids (specialist teaching and/or equipment, e.g. appropriate seating, ICT equipment).

The 2014 SEND Code of Practice gives 'Definitions of special educational needs (SEN)':

A child or young person has SEN if they have a learning difficulty or disability that calls for special educational provision to be made for them. A child of compulsory school age or a young person has a learning difficulty or disability if they:

(a) have a significantly greater difficulty in learning than the majority of others of the same age; or
(b) have a disability that prevents or hinders them from making use of educational facilities of a kind generally provided for others of the same age in mainstream schools or mainstream post-16 institutions.

The 2014 SEND Code of Practice, defines:

Areas of special educational need

Special educational needs and provision can be considered as falling under four broad areas.

1 Communication and interaction
2 Cognition and learning
3 Social, mental and emotional health
4 Sensory and/or physical

Many children and young people have difficulties that fit clearly into one of these areas; some have needs that span two or more areas; for others the precise nature of their need may not be clear at the outset.

Children and young people with an Autism Spectrum Disorder (ASD), including Asperger's Syndrome and Autism, have difficulty in making sense of the world in the way others do. They may have difficulties with communication, social interaction and imagination. In addition they may be easily distracted or upset by certain stimuli, have problems with change to familiar routines or have difficulties with their co- ordination and fine-motor functions.

The 2014 SEND Code of Practice states that:

All children and young people are entitled to an education that enables them to:

- achieve their best;
- become confident individuals living fulfilling lives; and
- make a successful transition into adulthood, whether into employment, further or higher education or training.

Schools must publish accessibility plans and local authorities accessibility strategies setting out how they propose to increase the access of disabled pupils to premises, the curriculum and information. These plans and strategies must be published every three years.

To ensure that pupils with an autistic spectrum disorder (ASD) have good access to the curriculum, the Teachers' Standards Department of Education 2012 states that:

A teacher must:

- set goals that stretch and challenge pupils of all backgrounds, abilities and dispositions;
- adapt teaching to respond to the strengths and needs of all pupils;
- know when and how to differentiate appropriately, using approaches that enable pupils to be taught effectively;
- have a clear understanding of the needs of all pupils, including:

  - those with special educational needs;
  - those of high ability;
  - those with English as an additional language;
  - those with disabilities; and

- be able to use and evaluate distinctive teaching approaches to engage and support them.

1 The inclusive school

A school that is educationally inclusive is an effective school. An educationally inclusive school has the following features:

- an ethos of inclusion that is understood by staff, parents, governors, pupils and the local community;
- achievements of all pupils are valued, recognised and celebrated;
- improving teaching and learning for all pupils is a constant concern to senior managers;
- the well-being of all pupils matters; their attitudes, values and behaviour are constantly challenged and developed;
- staff, pupils and parents treat each other with respect;
- senior managers put into place actions and strategies to ensure that all pupils make better progress.

Schools should offer an inclusive curriculum, in the broadest sense, that is appropriate for different groups of pupils. Each school should have appropriate systems in place to identify the needs of different groups of pupils and ensure that its provision meets these needs.

Essentially therefore, the five principles developing a more inclusive curriculum require a commitment to:

- value all learners;
- set suitable learning challenges for groups and individuals;
- respond to pupils' diverse learning needs;
- overcome potential barriers to learning and assessment for individuals and groups of pupils;
- make the best use of resources.

2 Inclusion for pupils with an ASD

Pupils on the autistic spectrum are mainly educated in mainstream schools with a minority being placed in special schools.

Adults on the autism spectrum maintain that the goal of education should not be to change their 'way of being' to make them into typical individuals, but to acknowledge and appreciate their differences and create environments in which they can thrive.

(NAS)

The guidance that follows aims to achieve the above.

Most children with special educational needs have strengths and difficulties in one, some or all of the areas of speech, language and communication. Their communication needs may be both diverse and complex. The range will encompass ... those who demonstrate features within the autistic spectrum....

(Code of Practice 2014)

These children may require some, or all, of the following:

- help and support in acquiring literacy skills;
- help in organising and co-ordinating spoken and written English to aid cognition;
- help with sequencing and organisational skills;
- help with problem solving and developing concepts;
- programmes to aid improvement of fine and gross motor competencies.

3   Definition

Autism is biologically based, and is characterised by a 'triad of impairments' (Wing 1996). This affects a person's ability to use and understand social communication and social interaction, and to be flexible in their thinking, behaviour and use of imagination. In addition, there will issues related to hypo- or hyper-sensitivity to sensory stimuli. There are also implications in connection with motivation and generalisation. It is widely recognised that pupils across the full ability range may have this lifelong disorder and many may have additional special educational needs.

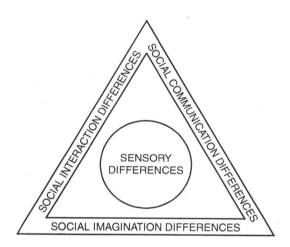

Throughout this book the term 'autism' or 'on the autistic spectrum' will be used to refer to all pupils who are at some point along the autistic continuum and therefore, will include those with Asperger's syndrome, autism, semantic pragmatic disorder, and pathological demand avoidance syndrome. These difficulties are seen as a continuum and the degree to which pupils are affected will vary significantly.

4 Asperger's syndrome

Asperger's syndrome is a developmental disorder that affects a pupil's ability to communicate effectively with others, fellow pupils or adults.

If you have Asperger's syndrome understanding conversation is like trying to understand a foreign language.

(National Autistic Society)

Some characteristics

- It is characterised by the four areas of differences described in the diagram above.
- It is considered to be on the milder end of the autistic spectrum.
- It mainly affects boys, most of whom will be of the average if not higher intelligence range.
- Language acquisition will be within the normal range, i.e. single words by the age of 2 and phrases by the age of 3. However, interactions with other children will be more difficult.
- The development of gross motor skills may be delayed. Toe walking is often observed.
- Non-verbal communication such as eye contact and facial expressions are not easily used.
- An obsession with a particular subject such as dinosaurs, trains often develops to the exclusion of anything else.
- A limited range of imagination restricts attempts at 'let's pretend' games (unless it is replaying a piece from a DVD) and the pupil will be more likely to line up cars in a particular way or organise information from their interest.
- A tendency to speak in a monotonous tone, which may be too fast.
- Finding it difficult to empathise with or be sensitive to other pupils' feelings.
- Older pupils will give a monologue of information about their favourite interest instead of carrying out a conversation. They will not realise their companion has lost interest.
- Being very literal in their understanding of language, which can lead to confusion, e.g. 'pull your socks up' may result in the pupil doing just this.
- Difficulty in understanding fellow pupil's non-verbal communication, tone of voice or the unwritten social rules, e.g. not standing too close to another person.
- A lack of understanding of humour, metaphor or sarcasm, which becomes increasingly difficult as language becomes more sophisticated with age.
- Pupils may become withdrawn but appear aloof or unfriendly.
- The condition can result in high levels of confusion and anxiety.

8

5 Social communication differences

Communication allows us to make our wants and needs known and to share our feelings, thoughts and ideas with others. It is what helps us to learn from relationships and make connections with the world around us and the people in it. Every pupil or young person with an ASD will have some degree of difficulty with communication.

The skills involved in communication

In order to communicate effectively we need to develop skills in a number of areas.

Processing and using verbal communication involves:

- the ability to listen and attend to relevant information;
- the ability to understand words, phrases and sentences;
- the ability to understand the literal and non-literal meanings behind spoken words and ideas;
- the ability to express our ideas with spoken words and to speak each word clearly;
- the ability to construct sentences and use English grammar correctly;
- the ability to use language for a range of purposes, such as requesting, commenting, questioning, discussing, and having conversations;
- the ability to use language appropriately in a social setting, i.e. what to say, when to say it and to whom;
- the skills involved in verbal interaction with others such as continuing the topic, monitoring topic shift and conversational repair (adjusting the content of the conversation if the speaker is aware that the listener is not responding appropriately).

Interpreting and using non-verbal communication involves a number of skills:

- engaging in 'joint attention', such as looking and listening together or sharing in the same moment or event with someone, with mutual enjoyment and meaning;
- using looking and eye contact both as a speaker and a listener;
- understanding and using facial expression;
- understanding and using spontaneous gestures and body posture to communicate or emphasise meaning;
- being able to interpret and use 'prosodic' features, i.e. how intonation, volume and rate of speech help to convey meaning and emotion;
- having the ability to take turns in social activities and conversations;
- the ability to initiate conversation and attract someone's attention;
- the ability to change the topic or style of a conversation to suit the needs or interests of the listener;

- the ability to understand implied meanings and read between the lines of what the other person is saying.

Language and communication difficulties associated with autism

Pupils with autism will have difficulties in a number of areas:

Understanding language

- There may be a failure to respond, or the pupil does not seem interested when spoken to. The pupil can be totally unaware that he/she is expected to listen unless specifically prompted to do so, e.g. in a group or whole class discussion.
- Unusual responses to auditory stimulation can result in sensory defensiveness. The pupil may attempt to block out confusing sounds or noises by covering his/her ears or by showing signs of distress.
- The vocabulary and grammar of spoken language becomes difficult to understand as it increases in length and complexity.
- Many pupils with autism are 'visual learners', i.e. they find it easier to understand visually presented information than verbally presented information.
- Information tends to be processed slowly. There is often a time delay between hearing what someone says and being able to formulate a response.
- Understanding of language is over-literal and concrete. Implied or ambiguous meanings can be confusing, e.g. sarcasm, idioms and synonyms.
- Confusion arises when people talk too loudly, too fast or use too many words.

Communication

- There is an absence or a reduction in the desire to communicate with others.
- The pupil may fail to compensate for the lack of spoken language, e.g. use of natural gesture, with the exception of pulling someone, or using his/her hand as a tool.
- The development of speech may be absent or delayed.
- The pupil may only communicate socially at a basic level, i.e. to satisfy a need or gain information.
- The pupil may develop some spoken language, but fail to use this for the purposes of communication with others.
- The pupil may be quick to echo speech or repeat 'chunks' of language spoken by other people, often without understanding the meaning.
- The content of speech tends to be one-sided and can be repetitive.
- The pupil may experience difficulties with appropriate conversational turn-taking.
- The pupil may accept or make approaches to others, but lack the skills to follow these through.

Strategies to help the pupil with autism to communicate more effectively

Helping pupils to initiate and respond to communication

- Being 'face-to-face' will encourage eye-contact and promote positive interaction.
- Observe what catches the pupil's interest and follow his/her lead and use this interest to encourage joint attention, motivate and develop learning.

- Teach turn-taking skills. Play turn-taking games and encourage more verbal pupils to take turns to speak and listen during conversation.
- Set up structured social communication skills groups to encourage pupils to take turns, listen and communicate with others.
- Help pupils to notice and interpret non-verbal communication such as facial expression and body language.

Helping pupils to understand what is said

- Say the pupil's name before communicating to help establish joint attention.
- Use physical prompts to gain attention and to guide the pupil through new experiences. Physical prompts should be phased out as soon as the task can be carried out independently.
- Reduce language, keep it simple, concrete and well within the pupil's level of understanding. Use key words and short sentences. Clarify ambiguous language for older pupils.
- Use a slower rate of speech to allow the pupil time to process the information.
- Be prepared to wait longer for the pupil to respond to questions or instructions – at least 15 seconds.
- Label objects, people and events. Use specific names and avoid words like 'this', 'it', 'he', 'she' and 'there'. Match labels or symbols to concrete objects or to activities while they are in progress.
- Ask fewer direct questions and increase comments, e.g. 'I see a car' rather than 'What is it?'
- Use visual forms of communication to support verbal language. These need to be appropriate for the pupil's level of development and can include real objects, pictures, symbols and visual or written timetables.
- Break down longer instructions using two or three simple sentences instead of one complicated one.
- Put information in a logical sequence within sentences and give instructions in the order they will happen.
- Direct the pupil's attention at an individual level rather than relying on whole class instructions.
- Interpret the pupil's actions and behaviours so they can hear the language they are unable to express themselves.
- Tell the pupil what to do rather than what not to do.
- Be aware that the pupil will have difficulty picking up on non-verbal communication.
- Help the pupil to identify meanings; are they:

    - non-literal (idioms, sarcasm, jokes…);
    - true or false;
    - real or pretend;
    - fact or opinion?

Helping pupils to communicate with others

- Be prepared to wait in order to give the pupil a chance to initiate communication.
- Interpret any attempts to communicate and be aware that the pupil is often communicating through their non-verbal reactions and behaviours as well as their verbal behaviours.

- As the pupil shows some acknowledgement of your presence try to 'intrude' into their activity, e.g. the pupil is sprinkling sand. Make it a shared activity, by, for example, dropping the sand onto the pupil's hand.
- Give the pupil reasons to communicate by not anticipating their every need.
- Develop communication through picture and symbol exchange, e.g. PECS (Picture Exchange Communication Scheme).
- Give verbal choices to help the pupil respond to questions, e.g. 'Crisps or biscuit?' rather than 'What do you want to eat?'
- Encourage the pupil to make requests using highly motivating objects and activities as an incentive to communicate with others.
- Model language as if you were the pupil talking, e.g. 'I want a drink' rather than 'Do you want a drink?'
- For pupils who are unable to answer questions, change them into statements, e.g. 'James made a ...' instead of 'What did you make?' or 'The boy is crying because ...' instead of 'Why is the boy crying?'
- Encourage the pupil to communicate in new situations and for different reasons.
- Be aware that the pupil may need to be taught how to ask for help and clarification.
- Encourage appropriate conversational skills; how to:

    - begin and end the conversation appropriately;
    - stay on topic;
    - introduce a new topic;
    - take a turn and hand over the turn;
    - repair conversation breakdown.

6 Social interaction differences

There is a wide variation in the level of social interaction observed, depending on cognitive ability, level of language skills, personality and situation. Difficulties arise owing to impaired understanding of the two-way nature of communication and interaction and how other people think and feel.

Pupils with autism may:

- seem to prefer their own company, showing signs of stress if others come too near;
- want the friendship of others but be socially awkward;
- find it difficult to look at the other person;
- not pick up the non-verbal social cues of mood, availability, social status;
- be over-familiar with teachers and strangers or over-formal with peers;
- not read the non-verbal signals involved in turn-taking in conversations;
- talk like a 'little professor' in great detail about their own, often obscure, interests;
- speak in a rather monotonous tone of voice, without varying inflection, speed or volume;
- be able to make friends initially, but fail to have the skills to maintain them;
- be vulnerable to bullying.

Strategies can be developed to support the pupil in a number of ways:

- If a pupil is extremely withdrawn and reluctant to engage with an adult, try copying their favourite activity in the hope or expectation that they will acknowledge your presence. For example, sit alongside the pupil spinning the wheels of a toy car and copy their actions.
- If contact with others seems stressful, a very gradual approach may be necessary in order to desensitise the pupil. Tolerating the physical proximity of another pupil may have to be built up in small steps.
- Using a small steps approach, gradually increase the pupil's tolerance of playing and working in proximity to others.
- Provide a workstation where the pupil may work for at least some of the time to reduce stress and minimise distractions.
- Practise new social situations with a sympathetic adult beforehand.
- Teach explicitly rules and conventions of conversation, e.g. how to begin and end, how to tell if another person is interested, how to take turns.
- Teach how to recognise a person's social status; unfamiliar adults and teachers expect to be spoken to in a different way from peers or family.

- Set definite limits on when, where and for how long the pupil may talk about a specific obsessional topic. Initially, use visual prompts such as a gesture or symbol to remind the pupil, fading to more unobtrusive methods such as a code-word or phrase.
- Model or film normal conversations and use role-play, giving feedback to raise awareness. Use videos, DVDs, film clips of real-life situations or soap-operas to provide training and make the rules explicit.
- Use a structured social skills programme to break down the skills of conversation into manageable targets.
- Provide more structure at break times, e.g. a support assistant may involve pupils in playground games with simple rules or in a lunchtime computer club.
- It may also be relevant to allow the pupil to have 'downtime', doing their chosen activity. This will allow the pupil to recover from the social challenges of school.
- Find another pupil/adult to escort the pupil with autism between classes. Have a simple plan/map of how to get to the next classroom.
- Have a clear anti-bullying policy, which is regularly monitored. Provide simple, clear guidelines on how to avoid situations and what to do if things go wrong.
- It may help to have a regular, set opportunity to get support from a particular member of staff, e.g. a mentor.
- Teach the pupil with autism particular behaviours to deal with specific situations, e.g. how to behave if someone is cross with you. The use of social stories may be useful in this context.
- Within the classroom routine, develop a series of 'jobs' that the pupil may do with, or for, other members of the class. Such tasks may be taking the register, taking messages, giving out drinks, handing out the books etc. Successful completion of these activities will also raise the pupil's self-esteem.
- All adults who may meet the pupil require some basic information on autism and the specific needs of the pupil.
- Keep at a distance that is comfortable to the pupil.
- Use a quiet tone of voice with the pupil.
- Continue with the interaction whether or not the pupil is giving eye contact.
- Use a form of communication that the pupil understands.
- Assess whether the pupil is likely to be able to understand and respond to a request.

Social communication groups

These should be small groups of three or four pupils with at least two adults. One adult is the leader whilst the other acts as a role model for appropriate behaviour.

The aim is to develop the appropriate skills for interacting socially and becoming a good 'friend' within a safe and secure structure. Pupils are taught a range of skills from sitting appropriately, being a good listener, looking at a communication partner, taking turns, to more advanced skills such as starting and ending conversations, negotiation, conversation repair etc.

Once acquired, the pupils should be helped to generalise these skills within everyday situations.

The group should meet regularly and skills are taught through a range of fun, rewarding games, activities, stories, role plays, modelling and discussions.

Circle of friends

This is a useful strategy, developed in the USA, for the development of social skills in pupils with special educational needs. The 'Circle' should meet regularly, with the intention of developing and implementing strategies to support the individual pupil at break and lunchtimes. If such a group is to be established, careful planning and management is necessary.

Social stories (TM)

These stories were the idea of Carol Gray from the USA. Individual stories are written for pupils, which will teach them the appropriate way to behave or react in a particular social situation. So, for example, a story about how to line up for lunch could be written for a pupil who always wants to push to the front of the queue. Social stories are also useful tools for the preparation for transitions, such as moving classes or schools. They are excellent for those pupils who understand simple sentences, and can also be written using symbols or photographs. There are published examples of social stories, but they should always be written on an individual basis, following the set formula.

Comic strip conversations (TM)

These are another idea developed by Carol Gray to support pupils' social understanding. Using thought and speech bubbles along with colours to denote different emotions, drawings are used to take a pupil through the different aspects of a situation that they have misunderstood. The aim is to help them grasp why people said or behaved as they did, and hopefully arrive at an alternative way of handling a similar situation in the future.

Nurture groups

These may be used as an extra resource for pupils to have the opportunity to develop social interaction skills within a small supportive group, but be mindful of inclusion issues.

Restorative practice

Restorative practice is intended to illustrate to an individual that their behaviour has consequences for others and making restitution for their actions. This approach may be difficult for some pupils with autism due to difficulties with social understanding and recognising the consequences of their actions. The above strategies may be more appropriate.

7 Social imagination differences

Impairments of flexible thinking, coherence and executive function associated with autism mean that pupils with autism may display a number of characteristics.

- They may have difficulty playing imaginatively with toys and equipment. Play may be restricted to specific interests such as lining up the dolls or cars.
- They may have difficulty developing 'make believe' games. Therefore the pretend game of 'Batman and Robin' could, in fact, simply be re-enacting an episode they have seen previously, which they are unable to develop further using their own ideas.
- They may become reliant on routines and have a need to keep things safe and familiar. Pupils may become anxious or distressed if there are any changes, no matter how slight they may appear, e.g. changes in classroom displays, daily routines.
- They may have difficulty creating something entirely from their imagination.
- They may have difficulty understanding another person's perspective.
- They may have difficulty making sense of everyday experiences, especially in understanding their social and cultural meaning.
- They may have difficulty generalising learning to new situations.
- They may take things literally and perceive things in definite black and white terms, with no grey area in between. The pupil who is told it is 'raining cats and dogs', for example, will expect to see exactly that, or if directed to 'go to the office', may do so easily but not know to come back again.
- They may have difficulty understanding abstract concepts. Those things that can be seen or touched will be understood, but for concepts such as 'furniture' or 'heavier', for example, it is difficult for pupils with autism to attach a visual representation in their head.
- They may have difficulty problem solving outside of cued rote responses.
- They may have difficulty widening their interests from their narrow obsessions.
- They may have difficulty remembering personal memories and events outside the context in which they occurred and making connections with existing knowledge. However, they often have an extensive memory for factual information learned by rote.
- They may have difficulty focusing attention outside their own areas of interest.
- They may have difficulty understanding 'cause and effect'.

There are a number of strategies, that will support the pupil:

- Use visual cues such as pictures and diagrams to support learning.
- Use a visual timetable to prepare the pupil for any changes in routine.
- Develop social stories to prepare the pupil for imminent changes such as a change of class or teacher.
- Use photographs to prepare the pupil for a new school, new classmates.
- Use similar formats and routines to increase familiarity and predictability.
- Simplify language and allow processing time.
- Provide frameworks such as storyboards and 'cloze' exercises to aid organisation and planning of independent writing.
- Teach the use of cues such as key words or pictures to aid recall.
- Allow time for the 'over-learning' and practice of new skills.
- Ensure that opportunities to teach the generalisation of skills are provided.
- Teach 'play' skills by modelling.
- Use the pupil's 'special interest' as a reward or motivator for working and good behaviour.
- Teach older pupils who have verbal skills the meaning behind common ambiguous sayings.
- Use flow diagrams to teach consequences of actions/cause and effect.

8   Sensory differences

It is evident from reading the personal accounts of people with autism that most experience difficulties in processing sensory information.

They may:

Be hyper-sensitive to sensory stimuli, for example:

- Sound – become distressed by the particular volume or pitch of sounds;
- Visual – be distracted by visual information/patterns/movements: eye contact may actually be 'painful';
- Touch – find touch, certain textures and changes in temperature uncomfortable/painful;
- Smell – find some smells and perfumes overpowering, no matter how mild they appear to others;
- Taste – dislike the taste of anything other than very bland foods;
- Proprioceptor – demonstrate overly rough play;
- Vestibular – poor balance, dislike of stairs, lifts, escalators.

Hypo-sensitive to sensory stimuli, for example:

- Sound – like to listen to certain sounds and vibrations close to their ear;
- Touch – not obviously reacting to pain and injuries;
- Sight – look intensely at lights/patterns/objects;
- Smell – like certain strong smells;
- Taste – enjoy strong tastes (both edible and non-edible!);
- Proprioceptor – clumsiness, toe walking, touching and fiddling with objects;
- Vestibular – rocking, inability to sit still, liking trampolines, lacking awareness of their own safety.

Pupils can fluctuate from day to day, or even hour to hour, between hypo- and hyper-sensitivity to certain stimuli:

- demonstrate behaviour that is related to sensory perceptual difficulties;
    - be able to only process information from one sensory channel at a time ('mono-channelled');
    - have a fragmented/distorted perception of objects, people and situations;

- be easily distracted;
- become increasingly withdrawn as they go into 'shutdown' due to sensory overload.

There are a number of strategies that can be used to help the pupil:

- Use observations to find out what sensory stimulation the pupil finds difficult/likes/dislikes and talk to the family/carers about this.
- Where possible, remove sensory stimulation that is distressing/distracting, and re-introduce it carefully and gradually, using a small-steps approach.
- Be sensitive to the fluctuations in sensory processing difficulties.

Try specific suggestions:

- Sound – use IPods, MP3 players, ear muffs, ear defenders, minimise background noise, use visual strategies to help pupils recognise volume control.
- Visual – use sunglasses, reduce clutter, use visual cues to aid focus.
- Touch – warn them before you touch, gradually de-sensitise and use massage.
- Taste – keep inedible things that may mimic food out of reach, introduce new foods gradually, try new foods when distracted/relaxed.
- Smell – avoid strong-smelling products, use favoured smells as a reward activity.
- Proprioceptor – develop motor skills through planned activities, teach rules around personal space.
- Vestibular – introduce new experiences carefully and gradually, allow for opportunities for movement activities.

9   Behaviour

Pupils with autism may behave inappropriately through lack of understanding rather than being deliberately 'naughty'. A number of considerations may be necessary in order to develop appropriate behaviour.

- Using autism-specific behaviour management techniques has been proven to be beneficial to behaviour management in general.
- Behaviour and obsessions are often symptoms of anxiety, so look for the underlying cause before reacting to the pupil.
- In order to alleviate some of the anxiety shown by pupils with autism, it may be useful to utilise their strengths.
- Try to provide a consistent daily routine or focus on activities with predictable outcomes: stability is very important for pupils with autism.
- Give examples of how to cope in certain situations. Think about providing a special flag or object to hold when it's their turn to speak/take part.
- Try to structure free choice activities for a pupil with autism. This is often a confusing and frightening experience for them and they may need to be gradually introduced over a period of time.
- Always use a calm, clear voice: pupils with autism may become excited and overstimulated by strong reactions or raised voices.
- Talk to others in the class about the difficulties experienced by pupils with autism. They may not fully understand the extent of their difficulties but it is important, so that they begin to understand the nature of the difficulty.
- Remember that although pupils with autism may appear to listen and understand what is said to them, they may not respond in the correct way. Target the pupil by using name or touch to focus his/her attention and by repeating group instructions to him/her on an individual basis.
- Try to vary the person who gives the instructions, so that the pupil learns to respond to a range of instructions/pupils/helpers.
- Pupils with autism may have difficulty anticipating the consequences of their actions. Make these clear by writing them down, or showing the consequences using symbols/flow diagrams.
- Use visual cues and clues – visual timetables are particularly effective in helping the pupil cope with what comes next.
- Keep language as simple as possible and be prepared to break down instructions into smaller components. Be specific when using instructions, e.g. 'Quiet please, sit down.'
- Use rewards for appropriate responses/behaviour and respond to attempts at communication.

- Try to teach the pupil that certain activities only take place in certain places (flapping, shouting, rocking) and give space for these or a special 'time out' for reward.
- Although structures and routines are vital to the well-being of a pupil with autism, they can also become a problem in themselves. Build some flexibility into daily routines – it can be something simple like a different cup, chair or song. Keep testing the boundaries in a sensitive and controlled way until the pupil learns that changes aren't always confusing and frightening.
- If the pupil begins to establish obsessive routines, then try and intervene before things get out of hand, e.g. warn them that equipment/books will go away in two minutes.
- Provide distraction-free work access, e.g. desk facing a blank wall not situated near a window. Be aware of the environment and try to identify triggers that may provoke undesirable reactions.
- Work on developing independence by choosing tasks/activities that have in-built success.
- Use visual timetables to teach work first, then play.
- Model appropriate behaviours and prompt them through new tasks, e.g. by a hand-over-hand method.

10 Whole school implications

Schools should give consideration to pupils with autism in their SEN policy. Schools are complex systems; staff working within them need to consider how to plan together to provide a consistent environment that reflects the pupil's particular needs and is conducive to their well-being.

When a pupil with autism joins a mainstream school, it is helpful to make a number of considerations in order to meet the needs of pupils with areas of difference, i.e. social interaction, social communication, social imagination and sensory differences.

The pupil with autism will encounter many people in school, who will need to have an understanding of their condition. These include:

- headteacher;
- SENCO;
- class teacher/form teacher;
- support staff;
- classmates;
- subject teachers;
- lunchtime supervisors;
- clerical staff;
- caretaker;
- drivers and escorts;
- visiting professionals;
- school governors;
- parent helpers.

In order to develop staff awareness:

- It is important that all members of the school staff be given information about the pupil and awareness training in autism (see section on Continuing Professional Development).
- All staff should understand the reasons for agreed strategies and the importance of a consistent approach.
- One person should co-ordinate information about the pupil, usually the SENCO. In a large secondary school, it is also useful to have one liaison teacher from each subject area.
- It is important that a member of staff with whom the pupil has frequent contact is identified as having a particular responsibility for that pupil, e.g. the class teacher or form teacher.

- Staff require information about the individual needs of the particular pupil or pupils with autism who attend the school (useful information can be gained from the parents).
- Pupils, and possibly other parents, may need to know something about the pupil with autism and understand how best to help him or her. Pupils could cover this in PSHE.
- Priorities for the pupil with autism might be different from those for pupils of the same age.
- Staff should decide together in which areas of school life the pupil might need different considerations/planning from others.
- The planning of space is important to meet the following needs:
  - social skills training;
  - a quiet place to go;
  - a safe place to be at playtimes and lunchtimes, as these are frequently the most difficult times of the day;
  - clearly defined space for personal belongings.

- A system of review needs to be established prior to the start of the placement – initially, this may have to be daily.
- Individual targets need to be small and may need adjusting weekly.
- Meeting to discuss Personalised Learning Plans (or equivalent) need to be held with the parents and pupils, to look at progress and set new targets.

The appendix 2 'What is an Autistic Spectrum Disorder?' provides a brief overview of autism that can be handed out to staff with encouragement to read the rest of the book at their convenience.

11 Transitions

Pupils on the autistic spectrum have difficulties with the process of transition. The extent of these difficulties will vary from pupil to pupil.

Difficulties will differ widely from anxieties around wearing new clothes, stopping an activity and moving to another (micro-transitions), to changing classes or transferring to another school or post 16 provision (macro-transitions).

Pupils may not be able to express their anxieties or even recognise them for themselves and so it is essential that staff are constantly vigilant and analytical of behaviour challenges that may be arising from transition difficulties. The issues should then be addressed in the most appropriate way to the individual pupil.

Teach pupils to say when they need help or do not understand.

Micro transitions

Micro transitions are those movements that may appear small or even insignificant but that may cause huge anxieties to pupils on the autistic spectrum.

There are a number of strategies to support pupils:

Visual timetables

All pupils will be encouraged to use a visual timetable that will prepare them for:

- What I have to do;
- Where I will do it;
- How much I have to do;
- What will happen next.

Visual timetables will vary greatly. Most pupils will have individual timetables, although some will follow a class timetable that differentiates for individual activities.

Pupils may have full day timetables, half day timetables

and even simply 'First.....then.....' visual prompts.

Visual timetables may use objects of reference, photographs, symbols or the written word.

Secondary school pupils should be reminded of where they are going towards the end of a lesson with the use of a visual timetable or diary.

Session plans/work schedules

Lessons and activities should be broken down into small steps, and visual supports used to help pupils understand what is expected of them during that session.

For example, a 1:1 session may be broken down for the pupil into 'reading words, counting, spelling, finished'. The pupil will be shown a session plan to demonstrate these using words, symbols or objects.

Timers

Some pupils may be assisted in moving on from one activity to another (especially when they are engaged in a high interest activity) by being given prior warning of the change.

A simple 'one minute warning' may be sufficient, whilst for others a sand timer or digital timer may be more meaningful and effective.

Also:

- Make it visually clear to the pupil what happens and where.
- Another pupil could be used to accompany the pupil with an ASD in transition.
- A map or visual photographs could be given of where to go next.
- The movement/noise of lesson transition can be frightening. Consideration should be given to the pupil leaving the lesson slightly earlier or later than the rest of the class.

Social stories

Social stories are an invaluable method of preparing pupils for micro transitions. They may be as simple as a sequence of pictures to prepare the pupil for what is going to happen, for example, 'minibus, library, minibus, school' for an educational visit.

Macro transitions

Macro transitions are those movements that would probably cause huge anxieties for any pupil, but especially to pupils on the autistic spectrum, e.g. moving class, moving to a new school/college, moving home etc.

There are a number of strategies to support the pupils:

Transition visits

When a pupil is due to undergo some planned change staff should work with the pupil and parents to help them prepare for this change.

- Wherever possible this should include making prior visits to the new setting. The number of visits made will depend on the individual pupil's needs and the practicalities.
- Visual supports will help them understand where they are going and what will happen there.
- Support the transition visits with an accompanying member of staff who knows them well.
- Photographs taken on the visit can be used for further preparation work, e.g. of the new classroom, with the pupil sitting in their new place.
- Maps could be compiled together with a walk around the building.
- Ensure that the receiving school/class has all the relevant information it needs in order to ensure a smooth transition.
- Information regarding successful strategies should be passed to the next teacher/ setting.

Visual supports

Pupils on the autistic spectrum are predominantly visual learners, therefore use visual supports to help pupils make macro transitions, e.g. photos, symbols or the written word, depending on the individual pupil's skills and understanding.

Social stories

Social stories will also support macro transitions, e.g. a sequence of photos put into a transition book or more complex stories which aim to help the pupil understand *why* the change is taking place.

Working with families

It is essential that schools work in partnership with parents and carers at all times, but it is especially crucial at times of major change for a pupil.

Ensure families are consulted about macro transitions and agree appropriate ways of working together to support the pupil.

Statutory transition planning for Year 9 onwards

- In line with the SEND Code of Practice all pupils will have a transition plan drawn up in Year 9.
- Full consultation should take place with the parents and relevant outside agencies.
- Involve pupils as thoroughly as possible, through a variety of means, including an adult advocate where appropriate.
- Encourage the pupil's attendance for all or part of the review meetings from Year 9. upwards. Recognise and respect that this may be very difficult for some pupils, especially if witnessing discussions about three years' time, which could heighten anxiety levels.
- Plan for how and when such information is discussed with the pupil.

12 Support staff
Roles and responsibilities

Support staff should:

Have a clear understanding of their roles and responsibilities:

- have a knowledge of their job description;
- maintain a professional demeanour with parents;
- be aware of school policies with regard to behaviour, anti-bullying, child protection;
- respect the confidentiality of information for all pupils.

Be aware of channels of communication within the school:

- ensure that information provided by parents is given to the appropriate member of staff – class teacher, SENCO;
- ensure that recommendations, communications or reports from outside agencies are passed to the teacher and SENCO;
- ensure that information given to parents is with the knowledge of the class teacher;
- ensure that there is a mechanism for disseminating information to support staff about school activities, e.g. daily diary, staff room notice board.

Be recognised as valued members of a team:

- participate in the planning and monitoring process.

Be encouraged to make use of their personal skills:

- share skills, e.g. ICT, creative skills.

Be supported with appropriate on-going professional development:

- observe and learn from other professionals in school and in other establishments;
- undertake training in school and through external courses.

Encourage the pupil's independence at all times:

- by developing independent work skills;
- independent self-help skills;
- personal organisation.

Teachers standards 2012 state that teaching staff should 'Fulfil wider professional responsibilities by: Deploying support staff effectively.'

The 2014 SEND Code of Practice, states:

> Where the interventions involve group or one-to-one teaching away from the main class or subject teacher, they should still retain responsibility for the pupil, working closely with any teaching assistants or specialist staff involved, to plan and assess the impact of interventions.

13 Support staff
Guidelines for working with pupils

Avoid	But instead...
Sitting next to the pupil at all times	work with other pupils, whilst keeping an eye on the pupil you are assigned to.
Offering too close an oversight during breaks and lunchtimes	encourage interaction with peers or allow the pupil to be solitary, follow his/her own interests and allow him/her to relax.
Collecting equipment for the pupil or putting it away	encourage the pupil to carry this out with independence, e.g. ensuring drawers are clearly labelled.
Completing a task for a pupil	ensure work is at an appropriate level and is carried out with minimal support (note any support given).
Using language inappropriate to the pupil	give short instructions at the pupil's level of development, with visual prompts.
Making unnecessary allowances for the pupil	establish what is required using appropriate strategies and have expectations that a task is to be completed.
Cluttered areas	provide a clear, predictable learning environment.
Tolerating undesirable behaviour	observe the pupil; determine reasons for behaviour and consider if changes can be made.
Making unrealistic demands on the pupil	ensure instructions are at the appropriate level and the goals are achievable.
Making decisions for the pupil	give the pupil opportunities to develop choice-making skills by providing structure and restricted choices.
The pupil becoming dependent on his/her support assistant	encourage independent behaviour and work.

14 Classroom management

Teachers are responsible and accountable for the progress and development of the pupils in their class, even where pupils access support from teaching assistants or specialist staff. The class or subject teacher should remain responsible for working with the child on a daily basis. Where the interventions involve group or one-to-one teaching away from the main class or subject teacher, they should still retain responsibility for the pupil, working closely with any teaching assistants or specialist staff involved, to plan and assess the impact of interventions. The SENCO should support the class or subject teacher in the further assessment of the child's particular strengths and weaknesses, in problem solving and advising on the effective implementation of the support.

(2014 SEND Code of Practice)

The needs of pupils with autism will vary greatly but the following may help to structure the classroom and reduce anxiety for the pupil.

Structure

- Pupils with autism need a structured environment that is predictable and offers routines.
- It is important to have visually clear boundaries for specific activities, e.g. this area is for work, this is for drink time.
- Structure the pupil's day by the use of a visual timetable, pictures or symbols, which show what happens at each part of the day.
- Diaries can be used to outline the timetable for the day for pupils with reading skills.
- Indicate changes that are to take place in the timetable.
- Free choice can cause anxiety: give restricted choice or direct, using visual prompts.
- Develop routines for times that the pupil finds stressful.
- Activities must always have a clear start and finish.
- The pupil should always know and be explicitly told (in an appropriate way):
  - Where I have to be;
  - What I have to do;
  - How much I have to do;

- The time I will be finished;
- What I have to do next.

- Provide the pupil with space for their belongings.
- Provide an area to work (possibly a workstation) that is as distraction free as possible, e.g. away from noise, windows, displays.
- Make available the equipment the pupil needs for the activity within this workspace whilst encouraging independent organisation where possible.
- Find a way of showing the pupil how much work has to be done, e.g. within the work area have a 'work to complete' tray and a 'work completed' tray.
- Use a timer to indicate how time is passing and that the work has to be completed within that time.
- Acknowledge anxieties and reduce pressure accordingly.
- Pupils are likely to need support to generalise new skills into different settings and in linking different bits of learning coherently into a whole.

Communication

- Consider alternative methods of ensuring that the pupil understands what is expected.
- Use photographs, symbols and drawings.
- Use photographs and videos to teach sequences of events.
- Do not tease even in a good-natured way – it will be taken literally and interpreted as criticism.
- Avoid negatives – tell the pupil what to do rather than what not to do.
- Do not overload the pupil with information.
- Use a slow rate of speech and give the pupil time to process the information.
- Avoid ambiguities.

15 Teaching

High quality teaching differentiated for individual pupils is the first step in responding to pupils who have or may have SEN. Additional intervention and support cannot compensate for a lack of good quality teaching.

(2014 SEND Code of Practice)

When teaching pupils with autism, to give them the best access to the curriculum through good quality teaching the following considerations should be taken into account.

- Provide activities that build on the pupil's strengths.
- Provide opportunities for breaks within an activity, which is relaxing to the pupil, e.g. playing music.
- Give clear rules and be consistent.
- Reduce the amount of language given; be precise and concrete.
- Tell the pupil what to expect.
- Always forewarn of a change.
- Mean what you say and follow it through.
- Consider a small-steps approach to certain activities, starting at the pupil's level, e.g. if going to assembly is an issue, start with a few minutes at first and slowly build up the time.
- Teach the rules, e.g. how to line up, how to sit in the dining hall.
- Indicate boundaries by the use of a red line (portable or painted on the ground).
- Teach waiting and turn-taking skills.
- Ensure you've got the pupil's attention – begin with his/her name.
- Do not assume that the individual is attending to you particularly in a group situation; gain attention, e.g., by touching the pupil's arm.
- Avoid confrontations with the pupil.
- Use the pupil's interests, 'obsessions' as rewards; include in the visual timetable.
- Give opportunities for exercise on a regular basis.
- Provide clearly defined breaks between structured activities.
- Consider the pupil's tolerance for other pupils in close proximity when considering seating positions – slowly develop the pupil's ability to sit more closely to others.

16   Accessing the curriculum

High quality teaching is that which is differentiated and personalised to meet the needs of the majority of children and young people. Some children and young people need something additional to or different from what is provided for the majority of children; this is special educational provision and schools and colleges **must** use their best endeavours to ensure that provision is made for those who need it. Special educational provision is underpinned by high quality teaching and is compromised by anything less.

(2014 SEND Code of Practice)

'The majority of children and young people with SEN have their needs met through mainstream education providers and will not need Education, Health and Care plans (EHC plans)' (2014 SEND Code of Practice). Whether the pupil with autism has an EHC or not they will access the National Curriculum, which will require differentiation through teaching strategies addressed throughout this book and more specifically below.

English

Speaking and listening

The impairment of social communication for pupils with autism will present great difficulties in this area. Detailed considerations are given in the relevant chapter (Social communication difficulties).

Reading

Pupils will have strengths and weaknesses in this area.

- Some pupils will have an interest in books and others will not.
- Language delays may hinder progress in reading but should not be a barrier to the introduction of the reading process.
- Pupils may learn letter sounds and names but further phonic skills such as blending may be difficult.
- In general, the visual skills of a pupil with autism allow them to learn words through a whole word approach.

- The high level of visual skills may enable a pupil to immediately recognise words without needing to decode, but this can mask difficulties with comprehension.

There are a number of strategies that can be considered:

- Develop interest through flap books, pop-up books, noisy books.
- Help pupils make their own books about their interests, differentiated according to their age and ability.
- Use repetitive stories.
- Use concrete examples, e.g. puppets or toy animals, to give meaning to text.
- Encourage relating the picture to the text.
- Use symbols to support reading, if appropriate.
- Ask questions to ensure understanding.
- A whole word approach may be more successful in preference to a phonic approach when learning new words.
- Pupils may relate more easily to non-fiction material.
- Use books related to their particular interest.
- Use computer programs as an additional resource.
- Use computer programs with apps.
- Develop understanding and inference through comprehension exercises.

Handwriting

- Clumsiness may affect handwriting.
- Use general good early years' practice to develop skills.
- Use lots of visual prompts, e.g. desk prompts to show how letters are formed.
- Use iPads with apps to encourage correct letter formation.
- Recognise that handwriting will be very difficult for most pupils.
- See Gross and fine motor skills chapter.

Independent writing

Social communication differences will impact upon independent writing, i.e. pupils will find difficulty understanding what is expected of them. Their difficulties with social imagination will restrict creative writing, by their inability to perceive something from another person's perspective and to develop imaginative ideas.

There are a number of strategies that can be considered:

- Ensure the task is within the pupil's level of understanding. Simplify the task if necessary.
- Follow up class input with individual input, use pictures or written prompts.
- Check understanding of the task and content of the lesson.
- Use real objects or pictures printed from the class input as prompts to overcome difficulties and prompt language with work recorded in the following way:
  - pupil gives verbal sentence;
  - the adult scribes the sentence (typed or written);
  - the pupil then copies the sentence using an iPad, AlphaSmart.

- If news writing is required, ask the family for photographs, objects from weekend activities.
- Cut up sentences that match well-known stories, for pupils to sequence. The sequenced sentences could be stuck into the pupil's book and captions added if appropriate.
- Demonstrate what is required, e.g. the adult types a sentence and asks the pupil to follow, with a sentence of their own.
- Use iPads to recall events, e.g. school visits, prior to writing about the visit.
- Use photographs to write captions for.
- Use the Clicker program with grids made using vocabulary the pupil can read and linked to the subject being studied in the classroom.
- Have an individual alphabet chart/word book/dictionary on their table.
- Use storyboards, picture sequences to provide ideas to write about.
- A writing frame can help with organising thoughts and the writing process itself; there are a number of software titles that may support this. Mind-mapping software can help to quickly get a number of ideas down quickly without worrying about structure or order.
- If necessary, suggest choices of sentences, characters, settings or activities for characters.
- Make use of visual prompts to aid writing skills, e.g. a defined area to write in, a red dot where the writing is to start.
- Make writing requirements measurable, by ensuring the task is clear, e.g. 'write three sentences etc'.
- Use alternative recording methods rather than using a pencil, which will be very difficult.

Mathematics

Pupils may have significant strengths in the area of mathematics but also some difficulties, which are related to the triad of impairments.

Strengths

- recognition and ordering of numbers;
- elements requiring rote learning, e.g. multiplication tables;
- basic computational skills that follow a set pattern or sequence;
- recognition of shapes.

Weaknesses

- using and applying computational skills to solve problems;
- generalising mathematical skills across the curriculum;
- understanding and developing concepts, e.g. bigger, smaller, longer, shorter.

There are a number of strategies to develop understanding:

- practical schemes such as Numicon, Cuisinaire are essential;
- the use of concrete aids, e.g. coins, counters, is vital;

- concepts such as 'more' or 'bigger' can be taught if lots of visual strategies and examples are used;
- consistency of the vocabulary used, e.g. always use 'plus' rather than different words with the same meaning;
- pupils should be taught to generalise their skills, e.g. once they can count bricks, can they count the same number of sweets?
- visual strategies to aid understanding and recording in all mathematical activities;
- use of desk prompts for number formation;
- use ICT to overcome difficulties with pencil skills;
- visual prompts at the top of the page to show the layout of work;
- use number lines with arrows to show + one way and − the other;
- pupils should have opportunities for lots of practice, repetition and the use of practical activities.

Science

Pupils will have strengths and weaknesses in this area:

- language difficulties will inhibit understanding of instructions, health and safety guidelines and concept development;
- topics within the pupil's experience, e.g. the body, will be easier to relate to;
- learning facts will be more possible than developing abstract ideas;
- topics that rely heavily on abstract thought will be more difficult;
- making predictions, testing hypotheses and answering open-ended questions may cause problems.

There are a number of strategies that can be considered:

- use symbols, pictures, written words to demonstrate health and safety guidelines;
- write instructions in order, i.e. as a list;
- use direct questions/cloze procedures/multiple-choice questions;
- use ICT equipment, e.g. video, computer programs, digital cameras, iPads;
- use concrete materials to illustrate teaching;
- use templates to support the recording of experiments/activities;
- adult help to support co-operative working.

RE, PHSE and citizenship

Difficulties in being able to distinguish between beliefs, facts and opinions may make discussion very difficult and potentially stressful. This will also apply to discussion in other areas of the curriculum.

Strategies

- use artefacts, photographs to develop concepts;
- match the task to the pupil's level of understanding;
- use closed questioning to develop understanding.

History

Reciting and memorising lists of kings and queens or dates may be relatively simple for the pupil with autism. Using empathy as a way through to understanding the human experience of different peoples at different points in time may be more difficult.

There are a number of strategies to support the pupil:

- for younger pupils, use photographs of themselves to sequence timelines;
- artefacts as concrete examples;
- videos, TV programmes;
- books and internet presentations, e.g. 'Horrible Histories';
- timelines in classrooms to demonstrate periods of time;
- visits with video or digital camera/iPad evidence;
- visiting theatre companies.

Geography

Some aspects of geography are more easily understood than others, e.g. through the use of maps. Pupils will find the recognition of countries more easily attainable on a globe. Understanding the concept of distance is more difficult, as is the understanding of other cultures and their way of life.

There are a number of strategies to support the pupil:

- use of interactive whiteboards, green screen technology;
- use a globe rather than a map for world issues;
- use TV programmes, photographs, internet search;
- build models to demonstrate other cultures.

For the above subjects there is a wealth of information on the internet.

PE

Difficulties with gross motor co-ordination may lead to fear of heights and being unable to jump over obstacles, the inability to manipulate games equipment. Social problems may lead to difficulties with turn-taking and team games (see the chapter on Gross and fine motor skills).

General considerations

In addition, a curriculum for pupils with an ASD should take into consideration the following:

- be pupil centred not subject centred;
- be delivered in a way that is accessible to the pupil;
- promote communication and interaction skills;
- teach life skills and promote independence;

- include a period each day of sustained physical activity;
- reduction of stress by:
  - the use of ear muffs, plain walls, screens, physical structure;
  - improving coping skills.

17   Secondary provision

In preparation for secondary school transfer, a number of considerations should be made in order to make a smooth transfer and reduce anxiety on the part of the pupil and their parents.

- Parents should visit a variety of schools (preferably within school time) and meet with SENCOs to discuss their child's needs before making decisions about their future schooling.
- Once a decision has been made, discussions should be held between parents, school staff and any outside agencies involved, to determine the provision required.
- Prior visits should be made to the new school. The number of visits made will depend on the individual pupil's needs and the practicalities related to visits.
- Staff from the receiving school may visit the primary school.
- Visual supports will help them understand where they are going and what will happen there.
- A member of staff who knows them well should accompany the pupil on the visits.
- Photographs or a video could be taken on the visit to be used for further preparation work, e.g. of the classrooms for various subjects and of key members of staff. IPads, smartphones or tablets are ideal for this.
- Maps could be compiled together with a walk around the building.
- The receiving schools should have all the relevant information passed from the primary school in order to ensure a smooth transition.
- Information regarding successful strategies should be passed to the next teacher.
- Training should be given to all school staff about autism and the specific needs of the pupil (the chapter Planning for Continuing Professional Development gives suggestions for this).
- Planning for lunchtime when a quieter area may be required to eat and take part in appropriate activities.

The 2014 SEND Code of Practice says that the following should being taken into consideration:

The reasonable steps taken to ensure that the inclusion of a child with autistic spectrum disorder who is noisy and constantly moves around in a mainstream secondary school is not incompatible with the efficient education of others may include:

- ensuring all possible steps are taken to provide structure and predictability to the child's day – for example, by the use of visual timetables, careful prior explanation of changes to routines and clear instructions for tasks;

- ensuring that the child is taught a means of communicating wants and needs using sign, symbol or spoken language;
- working with a member of staff on a structured programme of activities designed to prepare him or her for joining in class or group activities, for example by using 'social scripts' to rehearse appropriate behaviour;
- having an individual workstation within a teaching space where distractions can be kept to a minimum and everything needed for the work to be done can be organised in sequence; and
- ensuring that all staff are briefed on the warning signs which may indicate potential behaviour challenge and on a range of activities which provide effective distraction if used sufficiently early.

NB It should not be assumed that every autistic pupil 'is noisy and moves around a lot', but the above strategies plus others included in this book will support all pupils.

18 Assessment

The assessment of pupils with autism can be difficult and stressful for all concerned. However, assessment in some format will be considered necessary to show progress to parents, governors and bodies such as Ofsted. Formative assessment will also be required to inform and facilitate learning by identifying personalised learning goals and developing appropriate activities to meet these goals.

Standardised tests are often unreliable because the test situation is unfamiliar, the pupil may not understand the instructions and the unfamiliarity of the presentation of test material may cause anxiety. The pupil may not be motivated and see the point of making any effort, therefore testing may not always give a true reflection of the pupil's ability. It should also be acknowledged that the progress of pupils with autism is not always linear and the knowledge gains are not easily generalised.

Schools must weigh up (in consultation with parents/carers) the value of formal assessments. If it is appropriate to assess a pupil, schools can make their own arrangements for pupils with autism in internal exams. However, for public or national exams like GCSEs, special arrangements can be requested. Schools have to show that pupils need special arrangements through testing by a specialist teacher or an educational psychologist to determine which arrangements would be appropriate.

The following special arrangements can be requested:

- extra time and/or rest breaks;
- one-to-one or small group working;
- a quiet area;
- exam papers in different formats, e.g. digital format;
- support teachers to act as prompts;
- the normal method of recording, i.e. this may be use of a laptop.

The DfE 2014 Key Stage 1 Assessment and Reporting Arrangements state that:

Any pupil below level 1 does not have to do the tests/tasks. A pupil above this but with SEN who cannot access the tests does not have to do them. Assessment and reporting arrangements Key Stage 2, www.gov.uk give some guidelines for Key Stage 2 SATs testing.

Teacher assessment should be used if standardised testing is not appropriate.

The following strategies may allay some of this stress for internal and external:

- Support revision prior to exams, particularly if the students are off timetable.
- Prepare the pupils for examination situations by explaining what will happen, possibly through the use of social stories.
- Provide exam timetables.
- It should be explained to a pupil why taking exams are necessary, i.e. they will be needed to get a job.
- Sit the pupil in his/her usual working space (for internal assessment) or withdraw to a quieter area if this causes less anxiety.
- Give simple instructions with visual prompts if necessary.
- One-to-one working may be the most appropriate method of support for the pupil.
- Use a familiar support worker to prompt the remaining 'on task' work.
- Use a simple layout on a worksheet with specific areas marked to indicate where an answer should go.
- Define the amount of work to be done, break work into short tasks.
- Use concrete objects where appropriate.
- Provide the usual equipment for recording work, e.g. ICT equipment.
- Use a visual prompt as a motivator, e.g. work then reward.

A range of assessment tools are available for tracking SEN pupils' progress:

PIVATs (www.lancashire.gov.uk) is a system to inform target setting for pupils of all ages whose performance is outside national expectations and can be used to complement work alongside statutory Key Stage assessment.

CASPA (www.caspaonline.co.uk) is a tool for analysis and evaluation of attainment and progress for pupils with SEN.

bsquared (www.bsquared.co.uk) is a standardised assessment package to help schools assess small steps of progress.

19 Visual strategies

Pupils with an ASD are generally good visual learners and the following strategies will enhance access to understanding and learning.

Visual timetables

Pupils will benefit from the use of a visual timetable to provide structure, in order to reduce anxiety and promote independence.

Visual timetables can be used in the following manner:

- Select photographs, pictures, line drawings or symbols with a label, for each activity of the day, e.g. hanging up coat, sitting for English, individual work, playtime, etc. A large and small picture will be required for each activity. Laminate the pictures.

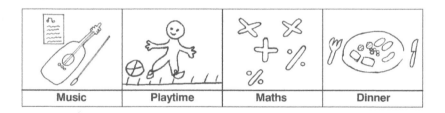

| Music | Playtime | Maths | Dinner |

- Encourage the pupil to remove the symbol card and match it to a larger picture that is placed where the activity will take place, e.g. in the story corner.

  - When the activity is completed put the cards in the finished box and accompany with the word 'finished'.
  - Encourage the pupil to look at what comes next.

- Eventually, the pupil can be encouraged to find what comes next independently and go to the task.
- Incorporate rewards into the timetable for completion of tasks.
- Pupils who have reading skills may move to a timetable or diary, in written form, with the activity crossed out as it is 'finished'.
- Changes to routines can be introduced by putting a new picture in the timetable. It may help to allow the pupil to take a familiar object to the new activity/event.

- Secondary school pupils may need a mentor to go through the timetable each morning and to note any changes to the routine.

Visual sequences

Pupils may need a visual timetable to support them through the day, but within that, they may need short intensive visual sequences to help them through specific activities that they find difficult. This could be times such as assembly, registration, toilet routines, lunchtime, changing for PE, e.g.:

Some parents may find visual structures useful at home, e.g. for the process of preparing for school.

Visual clarity

It is essential that tasks presented to the pupil with autism have visual clarity, i.e. it is visually clear what the task involves rather than dependency on verbal instructions.

- Each question/task on a worksheet should be within divisions marked by clear boundaries, e.g.

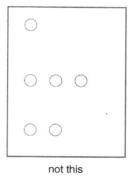

not this

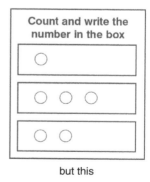

but this

- Ensure worksheets are uncluttered, i.e. containing the minimum amount of information needed for the pupil to complete the task.

- Make it visually clear where an answer should be placed, i.e. in a precise written or symbol form.
- Demonstrate elements of a task to the pupil within the session.
- Organise a specific place that is consistent for pupils to place finished work, e.g. a tray within the workstation or a box on the teacher's desk.

20 Gross and fine motor skills

Pupils with autism may have delayed development of their gross and fine motor skills, with difficulties that continue through their school life and are compounded by characteristics within the triad of impairment and sensory differences.

The following may be observed:

Gross motor skills difficulties

- an ungainly gait, when walking or running;
- walking on 'tiptoes';
- poor skills in PE related to gross motor skills difficulty, lack of understanding of instructions and the rules of the game;
- lack of understanding of the pupil's own positioning in space;
- dislike of other pupils in close proximity.

Fine motor skills difficulties

- difficulty with and reluctance to use a pencil;
- poor letter formation:
- disliking the feel of paper under their hand;
- limited understanding of the expectations of the writing task;
- difficulty with imaginative thought for a piece of creative writing;
- tiring quickly (due to low muscle tone);
- being anxious, which can also affect the quality of work;
- having difficulty working within a time limit or perceiving that the task is endless.

There are strategies that can support limited gross and fine motor skills:

Gross motor skills

- Encourage a wide range of outdoor play at home and school to develop gross motor skills.
- Encourage individual or small group activities to improve specific gross motor skills, e.g. balance, catching a ball.
- Support participation in PE, some aspects of which are more individual, e.g. dance, athletics will be easier.
- A defined area of the hall may be easier for some pupils to feel more comfortable.

- Encourage swimming.
- Rules of games should be taught using simple language and visual cue cards. Small group work may be more appropriate.

Fine motor skills

- Give opportunities to develop pre-writing skills.
- **Using the index finger in isolation** – finger puppets, making patterns in sand, popping bubbles.
- **Performing finger and thumb opposition** (touching each finger tip to the thumb) – rolling plasticine between thumb and each finger, popping bubble wrap between finger tip and thumb.
- **Eye/hand co-ordination** – holding a container to fill with sand, threading beads, holding a bowl whilst stirring with the other hand when cooking.
- **Developing a pincer grip** – putting pegs onto a line, picking up small objects between thumb and finger, using tweezers to move objects from one container to another.
- **Wrist rotation** – sharpening pencils, turning a skipping rope.
- **Finger strength** – squeezing water from sponges, rolling plasticine.
- **Crossing the midline** – with the left hand pick up beads that are on the right side and vice versa.
- Consider the use of pencil grips to improve the pencil grasp.
- Use a wide range of multi-sensory activities and materials when developing letter formation, e.g. chalks, felt tip pens, a variety of paper, white boards, using fingers in sand to trace writing patterns (be aware of sensitivity to certain textures).
- Consider the use of the 'Write from the Start' programme to develop writing and perceptual skills.
- Use a structured handwriting scheme. Consider apps on the iPad that help to develop letter formation.
- Give precise details of the space writing should fit into or the pupil may make their letters an inappropriate size.
- Avoid copying from the blackboard. Write the date and learning objective for the pupil. Use PowerPoint notes.
- Give cues, e.g. green dots to indicate where writing should start and red where it should stop.
- Be precise in how much writing is expected and how long it should take.
- Restrict the use of a pencil and provide ICT as an alternative, e.g. use of an AlphaSmart, laptop, iPad.
- Use the Clicker program.
- Develop a small steps approach to develop cutting skills. Trial alternative types of scissors (see the Peta website).
- Support may be required in technology lessons where difficulties with fine motor skills may cause problems. Specialised equipment may be useful.

21 Using technology

The use of technology can be a benefit to pupils in a variety of ways.

- Technology reduces the need for social or verbal interaction.
- E-mailing and texting provides an easier method of communication (this should not be at the exclusion of the development of social skills).
- Playing games programs with a peer gives an opportunity to show their skills and build relationships with others through a common interest.
- Software resources can help with the understanding of body language and help to teach social skills, e.g. 'Mind Reading'.
- Word processors allow pupils to carry out a project, make mistakes and correct them without stress.
- A number of changes can be made to the standard computer system to make it easier to use. Information can be found on the AbilityNet website that explains how to make changes to the mouse, keyboard and display options.
- Alternative equipment can be considered, e.g. 'Big Keys' keyboard, a range of mice, for those with fine motor difficulties.
- Touch screens are more easily accessible.
- A tablet computer also provides a light, easily accessed option.
- Word prediction may help with spelling or speeding up the input rate.
- Graphics and simple drawing programs overcome difficulties with fine motor skills.

22 Independence skills

Feeding

Children with autism often exhibit difficulties with eating and diet in a variety of ways:

- intolerance of certain textures of food, combinations of food and different temperatures of food,
- requiring routines for meal times, eating the same foods, sitting in a particular place and using particular plates etc.,
- an inability to express likes and dislikes or request a favourite food,
- manipulating cutlery.

Developing skills

- use appropriate cutlery, e.g. short moulded handles (IKEA cutlery), specialist adapted cutlery;
- practise spooning sand, shaving foam (depending on tolerance to substances);
- slice soft food such as bananas;
- carry out two-handed activities, e.g. peeling a banana, pouring from a jug whilst holding a cup;
- roll playdough, plasticine and cut into sausage shapes with a knife and fork;
- use non-slip matting, damp tea towels to stabilise bowls, plates.

Developing strategies to improve feeding

- identify foods to which the child is resistant and introduce new foods slowly by putting a new food on the table, then the plate, encourage touching, then licking the food before biting (this could take some time), distractions of music or a DVD may help;
- use social stories to address problems;
- have routines but try to have a little flexibility;
- introduce a simple activity prior to lunchtime;
- offer pictures of food to aid selection;
- give packed lunches, which cause less anxiety, as the pupil does not have to make a choice or be offered food they do not like;
- acknowledge that a noisy environment may be problematic and a smaller quieter environment may be more suitable.

Toileting

Toilet training may start later, take longer and be more problematic than with other children.

- develop a complete routine as children with an ASD like routines;
- make a visual timetable to match the routine;
- this should be in liaison with home;
- use the toilet rather than a potty;
- ensure the toilet is the correct size; a toilet reducer and footblocks may be necessary for a smaller child;
- have specific drawings/symbols of the process at the side of the toilet and also at the sink for handwashing;
- have specific times for the routine – a toilet symbol could be included in the daily timetable;
- use the child's name together with a symbol of the toilet to indicate that it is toilet time;
- carry out the whole routine even if the toilet is not used;
- determine if a reward is appropriate for using the toilet;
- distractions such as music or a book may help to encourage the child to sit on the toilet;
- ensure consistency between home and school with the routines to be followed, the language used, the techniques used, e.g. does the boy sit or stand to use the toilet etc.;
- encourage parents to dress their children in clothes that are easy to re-adjust, e.g. loose clothing that is easy to pull up and down.

Be patient, it may be a slow process.

Dressing

Pupils with autism may have a delay or difficulty with dressing skills due to a number of reasons:

- lack of motivation;
- sensitivity to labels, certain fabrics, new clothes;
- poor organisational skills;
- restricted gross and fine motor skills.

The following suggestions may help:

- Develop movements for putting on clothes, e.g. quoits over wrists, ankles and hoops up to the waist and over the head, before practising dressing skills.
- Play games to practise skills, e.g. dressing up with large clothes in the house corner.
- Backward chaining would be a useful method to teach the putting on of items of clothing, e.g. putting on trousers:
    - help pupil put trousers on up to knees; pupil pulls the trousers up independently;
    - help pupil put trousers on up to ankles; pupil pulls trousers up independently;

- help pupil put one leg in; pupil continues;
- pupil is shown how to lay trousers out and put them on;
- pupil sits and puts trousers on independently.

- Practise doing fasteners on dolls that have large buttons, zips and Velcro fastenings, do laces on wooden shoeboxes or tie up parcels.
- Encourage parents to dress their child in shoes with Velcro fastenings, trousers/ skirts with elasticated waists, school ties on elastic, clothes that are not tight (it may be necessary for uniform to have modifications to accommodate this).
- Younger pupils may benefit from having all their belongings, bags, hats in a particular colour or with a certain logo, in order for them to be found more easily in the cloakroom.
- Provide visual cue cards or lists to show what order clothes are taken off/put on, e.g.

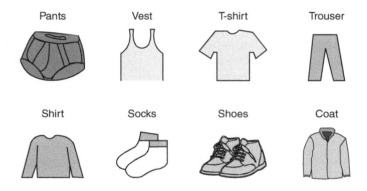

Pants   Vest   T-shirt   Trouser

Shirt   Socks   Shoes   Coat

- Encourage sitting to dress/undress, sitting with the back to a solid surface or holding onto a chair back to aid balance.
- Use T-shirts/sweatshirts with a logo/design on the front to help orientation of clothes.
- Give praise for effort when the pupil is trying to dress independently.
- Teach the pupil how to ask for assistance.
- Only help the pupil when he/she has tried for him/herself.
- Ensure the pupil does not miss out on playtime, etc. if he/she is slow to dress.

Older pupils

- Older pupils need to develop coping strategies to overcome their difficulties.
- Clothes need to be considered carefully to enable the pupil to have credibility with his/her peers.
- Consider how fashions can be adapted to make dressing easier.
- Adapt clothes with elastic, Velcro, e.g. cut the school tie and join with Velcro, adapt cuffs by putting in elastic to allow the hand to fit through.
- Use 'curly laces', wear polo shirts, jumpers with logos to help orientation, jumpers with raglan sleeves, wear belts with a magnetic buckle.

23 Self-esteem

It is important to acknowledge that factors associated with the areas of difference may present difficulties with self-esteem that are unique to the autistic spectrum.

- Through understanding others we understand ourselves and vice versa, which is difficult for a pupil with autism.
- Pupils will have difficulty recognising that people have their own feelings, thoughts, wishes and intentions.
- Pupils will have great difficulties in abstracting, feeling and thinking symbolically.
- Many pupils with autism are able to interact far more easily with adults than with other pupils.
- Pupils with autism are often totally unaware of social rules or may find them illogical.
- Most people with autism are able to learn social skills and rules eventually, but only clumsily and with great effort, i.e. social adaptation has to proceed via the intellect.
- Pupils with autism often have a need for solitude, a breathing space from social interaction.
- Relationships between pupils with autism and their teachers are sometimes impeded by misunderstanding and misinterpretation.
- Some adults misinterpret the behaviour of pupils with autism and see them as being intentionally rude or naughty.
- Some pupils with autism report that they are frequently in trouble, but do not know why. Staff need to understand that a pupil with autism is not merely a pupil that needs more discipline, but one that needs an autism-specific approach.
- It may appear that pupils with autism have a high level of egocentricity and that they choose to act in this way. This is not the case and they often don't understand their own feelings and behaviour.
- Anxiety and stress within the pupil come from living in a society where everyone is expected to conform to a set pattern.
- Pupils with autism are particularly vulnerable to the effects of bullying and are often genuinely traumatised by what others would class as 'mild' teasing.
- Pupils may find it difficult to access extra-curricular activities.

A number of strategies can be adopted to support the pupil:

- Avoid making immediate assumptions, but instead, take time to observe and analyse pupil 'behaviour'.
- Extend knowledge of autism through training, reading factual information, autobiographies.
- Help the pupil learn the social rules.

- Strategies to help to develop self-concept, self-image and self-reference will need to be taught through social skills work and circle time activities.
- Support the pupil if he/she begins to question his/her own difficulties.
- Give the pupil permission to have their breaks in the library or designate an office as a safe place in which to take refuge.
- Develop the understanding of peers through PHSE, circle time.
- Use circle time, social stories and social communication groups to help pupils build relationships.
- Monitor for signs of bullying and isolation of the pupil with autism and act accordingly. Support emotional and social development (this should include extra pastoral support arrangements for listening to the views of pupils and students with SEN and measures to prevent bullying) (2014 SEND Code of Practice).
- Give support and acceptance to develop a positive self-image.
- Use tightly structured questions and instructions to allow successful outcomes.
- Teach directly through social stories the concept of 'making mistakes'.
- Give opportunities to 'ensure that children with SEN take part in the activities of the school together with children who do not have SEN as far as possible' (2014 SEND Code of Practice). Pupils may require encouragement and support to take part in activities. Careful planning will be required for off-site visits.
- 'Schools should ensure that where practical pupils with SEN are represented on class and school forums. Colleges should ensure that students with SEN are similarly represented' (2014 SEND Code of Practice). Pupils/students will clearly need support to do this.
- Ensure good home – school relationships.

24 Pupils' views

The 2014 SEND Code of Practice states that:

> Children have a right to be involved in making decisions and exercising choices. They have a right to receive and impart information, to express an opinion, and to have that opinion taken into account in any matters affecting them. Their views should be given due weight according to their age, maturity and capability.
>
> (Articles 12 and 13 of the United Nations Convention on the Rights of the Child)

Choice making can be especially difficult for pupils on the autistic spectrum. The choice could be as simple as making a choice between a biscuit and a banana. Alternatively, it could be as significant as making decisions about their future after leaving school.

Helping them make meaningful decisions about their life may be achieved in a variety of ways:

- In order for this to be possible an appropriate method of communication should be determined.
- Teach and practise choice making in lots of different situations, through games, social communication groups etc.
- Use visual supports, e.g. pictures of two objects of types of food, to aid the choice making.
- Give real experiences of the choices so that they can make a meaningful decision, e.g. visiting two alternative college placements.
- Use social stories.

25 Home – school liaison

Early years providers, schools and colleges should fully engage parents and/or young people with SEN when drawing up policies that affect them. Enabling parents to share their knowledge about their child and engage in positive discussion helps to give them confidence that their views and contributions are valued and will be acted upon.

(2014 SEND Code of Practice)

There are a number of suggestions that may help to foster good home–school partnerships:

- Value the information parents give about their child.
- Share strategies that help to support the child.
- Inform parents when it is decided to provide a pupil with SEN support. The teacher and the SENCO should agree in consultation with the parent and the pupil the interventions and support to be put in place, as well as the expected impact on progress, development or behaviour, along with a clear date for review.
- Ensure that parents and/or young people are actively supported in contributing to assessments, planning and reviewing Education, Health Care plans (2014 SEND Code of Practice).
- Provide reports for parents before reviews.
- Parents should know whom to contact if they have concerns about their child, for example:
    - class teacher;
    - special needs co-ordinator;
    - headteacher;
    - special needs governor.
- Parental concerns should be listened to, acknowledged and addressed.
- Parents may be encouraged to become involved in the life of the school, e.g. as reading partners, helpers on school trips, school governors.
- Ensure parents are informed of visits from other professionals, e.g. educational psychologist, speech and language therapist, and receive any relevant reports.
- Consult parents before changes in provision are made.

- Acknowledge possible pressures within the family that relate to their child's condition.
- Use a home – school diary to allow school and home to create a dialogue about the child's home and school life, which will overcome restricted language skills (use photographs, objects from visits etc.).

26 The emotional aspects of life with a child with an ASD

Families respond to the diagnosis of autism in their own individual ways. For all families it is a devastating blow but for some the shock is tempered by the knowledge that at last someone has given a name to their child's difficulties.

In the months and years that follow, the families start the process of readjustment. Many of the emotions experienced will follow a pattern similar to that of bereavement and each family member may be at a different stage in the process of understanding and accepting the autism in their child.

- Initial feelings of grief are usually for the child that they thought they would have and now have lost.
- It is quite natural to want to search for a treatment or cure but it can be a depressing experience when it becomes apparent that there is no cure.
- Acceptance of their child and coming to terms with his/her difficulties follows the realisation that children with autism are first and foremost children but that they do need more help to overcome their problems.
- Grief may resurface at different milestones in their child's life, e.g. at secondary school transition.
- As the parents look to the long-term future there will be anxiety about what will become of their child.
- Parents naturally want to do their utmost for their child with autism but are also aware of the impact that this is having on family life. Having a family holiday or a spontaneous outing, such as a family picnic, will cause difficulties as it takes the child out of his or her normal routine.
- Accessing child care and/or baby sitters may be more difficult than for other parents.
- The lack of an obvious disability can cause misunderstanding of a child's behavioural challenges, e.g. throwing themselves on the floor in the supermarket if they can't follow their own routine.
- Extended family members may question the diagnosis or the approaches suggested by professionals, intended to support the child and its family, thus undermining the parents.

27 Siblings of the pupil with an ASD

Children who have a brother or sister with autism may need special consideration in school.

- Changes in their behaviour may indicate they are experiencing emotional difficulties that are related to issues around their sibling with autism, and they may require understanding and support.
- They may feel that things are not fair and more attention is given to their sibling with autism.
- They may feel resentful that they miss out on things that other families enjoy.
- They may feel embarrassed about their brother's or sister's behaviour.
- They may take undue responsibility for their sibling with autism.
- They may worry about their brother or sister.
- They may feel unduly protective towards their brother/sister and demonstrate anger at children who try to tease or bully.
- Some children may feel guilty about their feelings for their brother/sister.
- They may be teased or bullied because of a sibling with autism.
- They may need understanding from staff if their sibling with autism causes them to be late, forget PE kit, have homework disturbed.

28   Personalised Learning Plans

Once a potential special educational need is identified, four types of action should be taken to put effective support in place. These actions form part of a cycle through which earlier decisions and actions are revisited, refined and revised with the growing understanding of the pupils' needs and of what supports the pupil in making good progress and securing good outcomes.

> It is for schools and academies to determine their own approach to record keeping. But the provision made for pupils with SEN should be accurately recorded and kept up to date. Ofsted will expect to see evidence of the support that is in place for pupils and the impact of that support on their progress.
>
> (2014 SEND Code of Practice)

All teachers and support staff who work with the child should be made aware of their needs, the support provided and any teaching strategies or approaches that are required. This should also be recorded on the school's information system.

When planning for pupils with autism, it is necessary to take into consideration the four areas of difference, i.e.:

- social communication;
- social imagination;
- social interaction;
- sensory differences.

It is especially important that parents are consulted throughout this process and are encouraged to participate in its implementation. Pupils should also be encouraged to make their contributions to the process.

The following are pen pictures of a varied sample of pupils with autism together with sample 'Personalised Learning Plans'. These are examples of methods of recording goals, activities and support that will help the pupil make progress. These methods may be determined by individual schools, academies and local authorities. They should be reviewed termly and the responsibility of the parent, pupil and school should also be identified.

A blank sheet is included for use when planning in school.

Paul

Paul is three years old and has just entered a Foundation Stage class. His brother has an ASD but Paul has yet to have a diagnosis.

He has no language other than the occasional babbling. He is unaware of and lacks any understanding of class instructions. He makes little interaction with adults other than to briefly listen to one action rhyme. He is oblivious to the other children.

He cannot follow classroom routines and is resistant to requests to join in group time and will not sit with other children at group time even to drink milk. He does not play with any activities for more than a few seconds before running to another part of the Foundation Stage area, requiring a member of staff to leave the group to follow him to ensure his safety.

He will not tolerate sand or finger paint. He is not toilet trained and is wearing nappies.

St Mary's Nursery and Infant School			
Learning Plan			
Name: Paul **Date:** 1.3.14	**Date of birth:** 5.2.11 **Review date:** 18.4.14		
Nature of pupil's difficulties:	Social and communication difficulties. Unable to follow any nursery routines. Finds it difficult to sit for snack time. Cannot interact with adults. Finds sand and finger paint difficult to tolerate.		
Targets	**Strategies**	**Resources**	**Evaluation**
Social interaction To share an activity with an adult for a few minutes.	Say Paul's name before communicating. Use physical prompts to gain attention. Copy his favourite activity. Encourage sitting at a table, introduce a new toy, adult plays with it and offers it to Paul to take a turn with (hand over hand if tolerated).	High interest toys, e.g. car with flashing light. Marble runs.	
Social imagination To move to an activity when requested.	Introduce a picture of a child sitting for snack time snack. Have another picture in snack area to match to. Take Paul and the picture to the area, model sitting whilst looking at picture, give milk when he is sitting. Reward good sitting by giving a favoured activity next (identified visually).	Pictures of sitting. Pictures of snack. Picture of an identified activity he enjoys (put on visual prompt card).	

Targets	Strategies	Resources	Evaluation
Social communication	Introduce a symbol for a snack, use hand over hand method to exchange the symbol for a favourite snack.	Symbols of favoured snack food.	
Sensory differences To tolerate sand play.	Introduce a small bowl of sand, put in some small toys he likes whilst he is watching. Demonstrate picking out toys then encourage Paul to pick the toys out.	Sand, bowl, small toys.	
Parental involvement:	Try symbol exchange to request a favourite food (school to teach parent how to do this).		

Joe

Joe is five years old. He has just started in a Foundation Stage class (he was a year later than his peers starting into school). He uses single words to make comments, mainly 'book', 'no', 'Mummy'. He becomes very agitated before home time and will say 'Mummy' over and over again.

He enjoys reading books and playing games on the computer.

He can count and recognise numbers to 100.

He is unable to be involved in other pupils' play. He dislikes playing outside.

He finds it very difficult to sit in a group situation.

Some situations in school have proved difficult, e.g. going into the hall for assembly. He does not like loud noise and puts his hands over his ears to block it out.

He is not fully toilet trained and will urinate in the classroom.

Riverview Primary School			
Learning Plan			
Name: Joe **Date:** 16.4.14	**Date of birth:** 5.4.09 **Review date:** 18.7.14		
Nature of pupil's difficulties:	ASD. Finds it difficult to sit in a group situation. Finds noise difficult to tolerate. Cannot interact with other children. Urinates inappropriately.		
Targets	**Strategies**	**Resources**	**Evaluation**
Social interaction To take turns with a child (adult-directed).	Turn-taking activities with an adult, using key words to support, i.e. Joe's turn, Ms Kay's turn. Joe to take turns with another child, with the adult directing.	Roller balls. Marble runs. Lotto games.	

Targets	Strategies	Resources	Evaluation
Social imagination To accept use of the visual timetable to follow the classroom routines.	Introduce symbols to indicate group time and a reward symbol, i.e. read a book. Introduce to the group when a book is being read. Adult to give support (sit behind on the floor initially).	Visual timetable showing group time then reward. Reduce the proximity of the adult to Joe. Increase the time he is expected to sit in the group.	
Social communication To request books to read (favourite activity).	Introduce appropriate picture in a choice book, have two pictures initially. Model words, 'Read books, please'.	Pictures of books and other activities. Choice book (small photograph album).	
Sensory differences Sensitivity to noise in assembly.	Sit near the end of the row and have the expectation to sit for a short time initially. Judge the appropriate length of time to sit, only exit when he is sitting well.	Ear muffs.	
Independence skills To use the toilet appropriately.	Include toilet symbol in visual timetable. Take to toilet regularly. Take a book to toilet to encourage sitting on the toilet. Use reward card.	Symbols for toilet and reward.	
Parental responsibility:	Encourage same toileting routines at home and discourage use of nappies.		

Isaac

Isaac is ten years old and has a diagnosis of an ASD. He attends a large main-stream primary school and is working at above average in all areas, with maths being a particular strength. In class he can be fidgety and appears anxious, despite achieving well.

The difficulties that Isaac experiences are centred around the areas of difference and as he has grown older, the gap between him and his peers has widened.

Isaac wants to be like his peers and fit in with them but he does not fully understand unspoken social rules that surround friendships and relationships. He can become obsessive over particular peers and then tends to control what they can and cannot do. This leads to confusion, confrontation and physical aggression when the targeted peer tries to distance themselves from him.

Isaac enjoys taking part in various sports but struggles to understand the roles that people have and he can become verbally aggressive in these situations. He will dominate games and also take on the role of the referee if he feels that a rule has been broken and not dealt with. He is very competitive and has difficulty coming to terms with losing a game. These areas of difficulty can make him unpopular amongst his peers and Isaac does not understand why.

Woodside School			
Learning Plan			
Name: Isaac **Date:** 4.9.14	**Date of birth:** 2.2.03 **Review date:** 12.12.14		
Nature of pupil's difficulties:	Difficulty interacting with his peers. Finds it difficult to play games appropriately. Becomes very anxious in lessons.		
Targets	**Strategies**	**Resources**	**Evaluation**
Social interaction To understand that controlling situations and dominating peers can make him unfavourable to them.	Use social stories. Social skills group. Staff to structure activities at break times, giving specific rules and roles within the games.	Social stories. Social skills pack. Staff involvement in structured games and activities. Visual rules for structured games.	
Social imagination To know that he cannot win all games and activities that he takes part in.	Social stories. Create times for structured game play, initially with Isaac and an adult, then introducing one peer. Staff to structure activities at break times, giving specific rules and roles within the games.	Social stories. A timetabled slot to play structured games with an adult (and then a peer). Various, age appropriate games. Staff involvement in structured games and activities.	
Social communication To communicate to an adult when he needs 'time out'.	1–10 scale of emotions so that Isaac begins to recognise when his feelings begin to escalate. To seek out an adult and hand them a 'time out' card when he becomes frustrated.	1–10 emotions scale. An adult to help Isaac begin to understand his feelings, e.g. what would a 10 look like? 'Time out' card. Designated, quiet room within school that Isaac can get to quickly. All staff to be made aware of the 'time out' card.	
Parental involvement:	Parents to play structured games at home with siblings.		

Sarah

Sarah is a 13 year old with a diagnosis of ASD. She attends a mainstream secondary school. Every half term the school have a big learning day where all pupils are off timetable for a day. Sarah finds the change in routine challenging, making it difficult for her to access the learning. She becomes very agitated and unsettled. She refuses to go into the lessons and spends the day working on her own in her head of year's office.

Academically she is in a middle group for all subjects. Staff often complain that she shouts out random words linked to her interests in lessons. This is disrupting the other learners and her peers are becoming annoyed with her, affecting her relationships with others. Staff have spoken to Sarah and she often receives sanctions, however she continues to shout out.

She has found it difficult to make friendships at school and can often be seen wandering around on her own at break and lunchtimes. She will occasionally walk around with the member of staff on duty.

Northmore Academy			
Learning Plan			
Name: Sarah **Date:** 4.9.14	**Date of birth:** 1.1.10 **Review date:** 10.12.14		
Nature of pupil's difficulties:	Becomes distressed by changes in school routines. Shouts out in lessons and talks too much about her interests. Finds it difficult to form friendships.		
Targets	**Strategies**	**Resources**	**Evaluation**
Social interaction To develop conversational skills. To develop her ability to interact with peers appropriately.	Staff to organise structured lunchtime activities.	Encouragement to join clubs, e.g. computer, games, art, reading.	
Social imagination To accept changes to timetable.	Social stories. Preparation through looking at content of the day. Small group activities. Motivation through a reward chart, with reward at the end of each lesson. TA support. Use calendar.	Social stories. Access to smaller group. A member of staff to support. Reward chart with set of appropriate motivators. Use of a calendar to show changes.	
Social communication To wait for an appropriate time to discuss her interests.	Social stories. Visual talk/quiet card. Visual prompts. Allocated time to discuss her interests. Access to lunchtime clubs linked to her interests.	Social stories. Visual talk/quiet card. Time with TA to discuss interests during the day. Timetable of lunchtime clubs.	
Parental involvement:	Encouragement to join out-of-school clubs linked to interests.		

School Learning Plan			
Name: Date:	Date of birth: Review date:		
Nature of pupil's difficulties:			
Targets	Strategies	Resources	Evaluation
Social communication			
Social interaction			
Social imagination			
Sensory differences			
Parental involvement:			
Pupil involvement:			

29 Transition to adulthood

> Pupils should be supported … in decisions about their transition to adult life. They should also be involved in discussions about the schools and colleges they would like to attend. EHC plans should reflect this important ambition.
> (Special Educational Needs and Disability
> 2014 SEND Code of Practice)

Local authorities, education providers and their partners should work together to help children and young people achieve successful long-term outcomes, such as getting a job or going into higher education, being able to make choices about their support and where they live, and making friends and participating in society. Raising aspirations is crucial if young people are to achieve these goals.

Planning needs to start early on, from Year 9 in school at the latest, pupils with an EHCP (and those without) should have a review during which planning for the future is discussed.

The following should be considered:

- current skills and interests;
- future education;
- employment;
- housing.

It is important that the following considerations are made to allow the correct provision to be made for the young person's future.

- Some pupils may lack the cognitive ability to make decisions about their future although this should not be the case with those with Asperger's syndrome.
- The accessible method of communication for the pupil should be taken into consideration, e.g. pictures rather than too much speech and inappropriate language.
- Pupils will have difficulty considering the possibilities for their future and dealing with change.
- Role models with the same interests may provide ideas.

- Providing experiences may make possibilities more real, e.g. work experience, further education placements, types of accommodation.
- The Children and Families Bill gives significant rights directly to young people once they reach 16. When a young person is over 16, local authorities and other agencies should normally engage directly with the young person, ensuring that as part of the planning process, they identify the relevant people who should be involved, and how to involve them.

For those moving to Further Education the 2014 SEND Code of Practice suggests:

- the involvement of staff from the college's learning support team in the school-based transition reviews;
- an orientation period during the summer holidays, to enable the student to find his way around the college campus and meet the learning support staff;
- opportunities to practise travelling to and from college;
- the development of an individual learning programme outlining longer term goals covering all aspects of learning and development, with shorter term targets to meet the goals;
- supported access to taster sessions over a first year in college;
- a more detailed assessment of the young person's needs and wishes provided by learning support tutors during a 'taster' year;
- staff development to ensure an understanding of the student's particular method of communication;
- use of expertise in access technology to identify appropriate switches, communication boards to facilitate the student's involvement in an entry level course;
- courses normally covered in one year planned over two years to meet the young person's learning needs.

When a young person with an Education Health and Care plan takes up a place in higher education, their EHC plan will cease. Local authorities should plan a smooth transition to the Higher Education institution concerned (and, where applicable, to the new local authority area) before ceasing to maintain the young person's plan. Once the young person's place has been confirmed at the Higher Education institution, the local authority **must** (with the young person's permission) pass a copy of their EHC plan to the relevant member of staff.

30 Planning for Continuing Professional Development (CPD)

With a number of children entering school with autism, it is more important than ever that all staff (including teaching assistants, lunchtime supervisors, drivers and support staff) feel able to meet their needs. The provision of carefully tailored CPD will help to build colleagues' confidence in this area and develop a consistent approach through the school.

An outline plan of CPD sessions might incorporate objectives such as ensuring that colleagues have:

- a sound knowledge of the issues involved (the difficulties encountered by children with autism, in different lessons, in the playground, outside school);
- the ability to identify children with autism;
- the confidence to ask experienced colleagues for help and advice;
- a range of strategies to meet individual needs and reduce barriers to learning.

Format of CPD

The method of delivering professional development will depend on particular factors relating to the school as a whole, and to individual teachers and TAs. The opportunity to learn more about children with autism will be welcomed by colleagues who recognise children they teach, support or supervise as having difficulties – the issues are then immediately relevant. But it's also important for staff to appreciate that there may be pupils who experience difficulties but who have not been formally identified; for these children, basic good practice can make a significant difference to how well they can access learning.

There are many different formats of CPD to consider:

- **Whole-staff training during a CPD day, or staff meeting.** You may choose to invite an 'expert speaker', a colleague from a neighbouring school (perhaps a specialist school for autism), a member of your LA pupil support team, an educational psychologist or a speech and language therapist. If you do choose this option, be sure to brief the speaker adequately: he or she needs to know the precise range and nature of pupils with autism in your school; what if any, interventions are in place; details of previous training received by staff.

A school's SENCo is often the best person to plan and deliver such training however, as he or she knows the school, the staff and the children, and can ensure that information and advice offered is relevant and appropriate. Such a person can also build in opportunities for follow-up and on-going development. Be 'in it together'; mutual vulnerability can be a powerful medium for exploring how changes to practice can result in positive developments.

- **Phase or pastoral group training:** scheduled sessions for TAs, EYFS staff, learning support team etc. This may be focused on learning to use a specific approach or resource such as PECS (Picture Exchange Communication System), Makaton or Symbol Maker.
- **Sharing best practice** (sometimes referred to as 'joint practice development' – JPD): this is more about working together than about transferring knowledge or tips from one educator to another. Activities such as peer observation and shared planning can help to develop a sense of common purpose among staff.
- **Individual mentoring/coaching:** this can be particularly useful where a colleague is teaching a child with significant needs and has no previous experience of dealing with autism.
- **Individual study:** colleagues who strive to make good provision for autistic pupils can become very interested in finding out more, even developing expertise in the field. Pursuing a course of study at university, attending a PECs course or locally provided training should be encouraged and supported – with the proviso that there will be some form of dissemination to colleagues. This course of action can be particularly beneficial to TAs tasked with delivering intervention programmes and/or supporting individual children with autism.
- **Encourage professional reading** in small groups or individually. Place new relevant books (including this one!) in the staffroom library; seek out and share articles and research studies as food for thought, as well as reviews of useful resources. Perhaps devote five minutes of meeting time to highlight why you have selected particular reading matter. Encourage staff to contribute to this process too. Perhaps use social networking or your school's virtual learning environment to facilitate it.

31 Evaluating and following up CPD

Whichever mode of CPD is delivered (you may choose a mixed menu), it's important to evaluate its effectiveness and plan for on-going development. Consider a short evaluation sheet for staff to complete after a training session on autism, including their suggestions and requests for further development opportunities.

Taking this information into consideration, you can then plan follow-up work to consolidate and build on the training delivered. This provides good accountability evidence for senior managers and Ofsted, and demonstrates the school's (and SENCO's) effectiveness. Ideas for follow-up activities are suggested below:

- a regular 'surgery' where teachers and TAs can seek advice from the SENCO or outreach support teachers;
- optional 'advanced' CPD for interested staff;
- opportunities for teachers to observe intervention programmes – in your own school or elsewhere;
- a working party to trial a new approach;
- an action-research project to test an intervention and report back to staff on its effectiveness;
- classroom observations by the SENCO to monitor colleagues' effectiveness in providing for the needs of children with autism;
- detailed tracking of children with autism to monitor progress and evaluate strategies being used to support them.

A brief overview of autism CPD can be found in Appendix 2.

Social communication

Pupils may have difficulty understanding and using:

- the initiation and maintenance of conversations;
- language content and structure;
- volume of speech, intonation and pitch;
- turn-taking in conversations;
- non-verbal communication: facial expression, body language, gesture;
- eye contact.

Some tips to support the pupil:

- keep language clear and simple;
- give time for the pupil to respond;
- teach turn-taking skills;
- use visual prompts;
- avoid sarcasm.

Social interaction

Pupils may have poor social understanding and have difficulties with:

- developing and maintaining relationships (pupils may prefer to be solitary or want to have friendships but lack the skills);
- understanding another person's feelings/perspective;
- working as part of a pair/group/team;
- using appropriate behaviour towards others (peers and adults);
- understanding 'social rules'.

Some tips to support the pupil:

- teach how to play with an adult and then with a peer;
- encourage supported social interaction;
- teach social skills;
- use social stories;
- use circle of friends/buddies.

Social imagination/flexibility of thought

Pupils may:

- have difficulty with understanding abstract concepts, e.g. 'more', 'faith', 'history';
- have difficulty with work involving creative thinking, e.g. story writing;
- dislike changes in routine;
- have a restricted range of interests;
- display stereotyped body movements, e.g. flapping, rocking;
- find difficulty transferring skills.

> **Some tips to support the pupil:**
>
> - use a visual timetable/diary to show the structure of the day;
> - use a calendar to prepare for change;
> - give warning of changes – timers/count down;
> - use visual cues to develop understanding;
> - provide structures/choices to support creative work;
> - teach generalisation from one situation to another.

Sensory difficulties

> **Pupils with autism may have sensory differences resulting in:**
>
> - hyper-sensitivity to sensory information, e.g. noise, light, textures;
> - hypo-sensitivity to sensory information, e.g. pain, hunger;
> - being mono-channelled;
> - easily distracted;
> - their sensitivity may fluctuate.

Motivation

> **Pupils with autism may not have the same motivation as others, owing to difficulties with social understanding. Support them by:**
>
> - observing the pupil to establish what they are interested in to use as an appropriate reward;
> - including the reward in the visual timetable to reward a completed task;
> - rewarding frequently.

Strengths

> **Pupils with autism will have a variety of strengths, varying from person to person, which will help to access the curriculum, including:**
>
> - ability to process visual information;
> - good use of ICT;
> - ability to focus on detail;
> - ability to concentrate on an activity of interest;
> - good at learning rote information.

Autism is a lifelong disability but there are many strategies that parents, professionals and the pupils themselves can use to manage the difficulties presented.

Further reading and useful contacts

The following publications will help in furthering the understanding and therefore support for a pupil with autism.

Autobiographies

Title	Author	Publisher	ISBN number
Martian in the Playground	Clare Sainsbury	Sage Publications	978 187394208 6
Asperger Syndrome, the Universe and Everything	Kenneth Hall	Jessica Kingsley	978 185302930 1
Freaks, Geeks and Asperger Syndrome	Luke Jackson	Jessica Kingsley	978 184310098 0
A Real Person	Gunilla Gerland	Souvenir Press	0 28563398 8
The Way I See It	Temple Grandin	Future Horizons	978 1 93256572 0
Little Rainman	Karen L. Simmons	Future Horizons	1 88547729 5

Social skills

Title	Author	Publisher	ISBN number
Personal Hygiene. What's that got to do with me?	Pat Crissey	Jessica Kingsley	978 184310796 5
Groupwork for Children with Autism Spectrum Disorder	Howe, Old, Eggett and Davidson	Speechmark	978 086388594 5
The New Social Story Book	Carol Gray	Future Horizons	978 193527405 6
Social Stories for Kids in Conflict	John Ling	Speechmark	978 086388760 4
Comic Strip Conversations	Carol Gray	Future Horizons	978 188547722 4
The Hidden Curriculum	Myles, Trautman and Schelvan	Autsim Asperger Publishing Company	1 93128260 9

(Continued)

Title	Author	Publisher	ISBN number
Social Skills for Teenagers and Adults with Asperger Syndrome	Nancy J. Patrick	Jessica Kingsley	978 184310876 4
Incorporating Social Goals in the Classroom	Rebecca A. Moyes	Jessica Kingsley	978 185302967 7
The Asperkid's Secret Book of Social Rules	Jennifer Cook O'Toole	Jessica Kingsley	978 184905915 2
Talkabout	Alex Kelly	Speechmark	978 86388323 1
Talkabout Activities	Alex Kelly	Speechmark	978 086388404 7
Talkabout Relationships	Alex Kelly	Speechmark	978 086388405 4
Talkabout Teenagers	Alex Kelly & Brian Sains	Speechmark	978 086388782 6
Social Skills Programmes	Maureen Aarons & Tessa Gittens	Speechmark	978 086388310 1
Taking Care of Myself	Mary Wrobel	Future Horizons	1 88547794 5

General

Title	Author	Publisher	ISBN number
The ASD Workbook	Penny Kershaw	Jessica Kingsley	978 184905195 8
Asperger Syndrome in Adolescence	Lianne Holliday Willey	Jessica Kingsley	978 184310742 2
Sensory Perception Issues in Autism and Asperger Syndrome	Olga Bogdashina	Jessica Kingsley	978 184310166 6
Teaching Young Children with Autism Spectrum Disorders to Learn	Liz Hannah	National Autistic Society	1 899280 32 4
Practical Behaviour Management Solutions for Children and Teens with Autism	Linda Miller	Jessica Kingsley	978 184905038 8
Behavioural Concerns & Autistic Spectrum Disorders	Clements & Zarkowska	Jessica Kingsley	978 185302742 0
The New Social Story Book	Carol Gray	Future Horizons	978 193527405 6
Special Educational Needs (SEND) Code of Practice 2014	Department of Education	www.gov.uk	
Teachers Standards, 2012	Department of Education	www. education. gov.uk/ schools	
Write from the Start	Addy and Teodorescu	LDA	0742401618, 978074201617

Resources to support the pupil

Ability Net www.abilitynet.org.uk gives suggestions for the use of ICT
Apps, Accessories and Activities from HelpKidzlearn Inclusive Technology: helpkidzlearn.com
Autism Education Trust Competency Framework www.aettraininghubs.org.uk
Clicker software from www.cricksoft.com.uk
Peta scissors from www.peta-uk.com
Taskmaster www.taskmasteronline.co.uk for pencil grips, scissors
The National Autistic Society, 393 City Road, London EC1V 1NG. Tel 0207 833 2299 email@nas.org.uk

Appendix 1
Some professionals who may be involved with the pupil

Professional	Personnel and contact number
Special Needs Adviser	
Educational Psychologist	
Specialist Outreach Teacher for ASD	
Speech and Language Therapist	
Special Educational Needs Support Service	
Hearing Impairment Service	
School Nurse	
Occupational Therapist	
Social Worker	
Educational Welfare Officer	
Multi-agency link team	
Visual Impairment Service	

Appendix 2
What is an autistic spectrum disorder?

The following gives a brief overview of an Autistic Spectrum Disorder.

The term autistic spectrum disorder (ASD) is a broad term used to describe pupils with a range of difficulties such as Asperger's syndrome, autism, semantic pragmatic disorder, and pathological demand avoidance syndrome. These difficulties are seen as a continuum and the degree to which pupils are affected will vary significantly. An ASD is biologically based, can affect pupils across the full cognitive range and may be present alongside other disabilities/difficulties.

There are three key areas of impairment associated with ASD: social communication, social interaction and social imagination.

Social communication

> **Pupils may have difficulty understanding and using:**
>
> - the initiation and maintenance of conversations;
> - language content and structure;
> - volume of speech, intonation and pitch;
> - turn-taking in conversations;
> - non-verbal communication: facial expression, body language, gesture;
> - eye contact.

> **Some tips to support the pupil:**
>
> - keep language clear and simple;
> - give time for the pupil to respond;
> - teach turn-taking skills;
> - use visual prompts;
> - avoid sarcasm.

Social interaction

Pupils may have poor social understanding and have difficulties with:

- developing and maintaining relationships (pupils may prefer to be solitary or want to have friendships but lack the skills);
- understanding another person's feelings/perspective;
- working as part of a pair/group/team;
- using appropriate behaviour towards others (peers and adults);
- understanding 'social rules'.

Some tips to support the pupil:

- teach how to play with an adult and then with a peer;
- encourage supported social interaction;
- teach social skills;
- use Social Stories;
- use Circle of friends/buddies;

Social imagination/flexibility of thought

Pupils may

- have difficulty with understanding abstract concepts, e.g. 'more, faith, history';
- have difficulty with work involving creative thinking, e.g. story writing;
- dislike changes in routine;
- have a restricted range of interests;
- display stereotyped body movements, e.g. flapping, rocking;
- find difficulty transferring skills.

Some tips to support the pupil:

- use a visual timetable/diary to show the structure of the day;
- use a calendar to prepare for change;
- give warning of changes – timers/count down;
- use visual cues to develop understanding;
- provide structures/choices to support creative work;
- teach generalisation from one situation to another.

Sensory difficulties

Pupils with an ASD may have sensory difficulties resulting in:

- hyper-sensitivity to sensory information, e.g. noise, light, textures;
- hypo-sensitivity to sensory information, e.g. pain, hunger;
- being mono-channelled;
- easily distracted;
- their sensitivity may fluctuate.

Motivation

Pupils with an ASD may not have the same motivation as others, owing to difficulties with social understanding. Support them by:

- observing the pupil to establish what they are interested in to use as an appropriate reward;
- including the reward in the visual timetable to reward a completed task;
- rewarding frequently.

Strengths

Pupils with an ASD will have a variety of strengths, varying from person to person, which will help to access the curriculum, including:

- ability to process visual information;
- good use of ICT;
- ability to focus on detail;
- ability to concentrate on an activity of interest;
- good at learning rote information.

ASD is a lifelong disability but there are many strategies that parents, professionals and the pupils themselves can use to manage the difficulties presented.